MA

# WITHDRAWN

*You Don't Really Know Me*

# YOU DON'T REALLY KNOW ME

*Why Mothers & Daughters Fight and How Both Can Win*

## TERRI APTER

**W. W. NORTON & COMPANY**
*New York · London*

# To Miranda & Julia

For information about permission to reproduce selections from this book,
write to Permissions, W. W. Norton & Company, Inc., 500 Fifth Avenue,
New York, NY 10110

Manufacturing by Quebecor World, Fairfield
Book design by Charlotte Staub
Production manager: Anna Oler

Library of Congress Cataloging-in-Publication Data

Apter, T. E.
    You don't really know me : why mothers and daughters fight and how
both can win / Terri Apter.— 1st ed.
        p. cm.
Includes bibliographical references and index.
    **ISBN 0-393-05758-5**
    1. Mothers and daughters—Psychology.  I. Title.
    HQ755.85 .A67 2004
    306.874'3—dc22

                                                                        2003024322

W. W. Norton & Company, Inc.
500 Fifth Avenue, New York, N.Y. 10110
www.wwnorton.com

W. W. Norton & Company Ltd.
Castle House, 75/76 Wells Street, London W1T 3QT

1 2 3 4 5 6 7 8 9 0

# Contents

# *Acknowledgments*

**A BOOK ABOUT** the passionate arguments that bring mother and daughter closer together could only be written with the contribution of people willing to expose their anger, confusion, understanding, and love. To the fifty-six mother/daughter pairs whose heated negotiations are described in this book, I owe my greatest debt. Their generosity, patience, and humor as collaborators in my research were remarkable, and my greatest hope is that I have done them justice.

From the beginning I have had unstinting encouragement from my agent, Meg Ruley, and my editor, Jill Bialosky. Meg's enthusiasm could lift anyone above the slumps of self-doubt. Jill's clear vision of the project helped me focus, and her own passionate views of daughtering and mothering provided inspiration. With my sister, Marion Quinn, I began a conversation about mothers and daughters at about the age of eight, and we've continued ever since. I cannot imagine thinking about these things outside of a context in which we talk, constantly. Nancy Chodorow has acted as a supreme sounding board for radical departures from established theory. Carol Gilligan's warmth and interest were sustaining at crucial stages in both the thinking and the writing. Ruthellen Josselson provided assurance that there is always one step further to go in describing the mother/daughter bond. Michelle Spring and Mary Hamer were on call to analyze another detail and explore another perspective. Anna Baldwin persisted in her imaginative suggestions for developing the theme of mother/daughter conflict, even in the midst of her own pressing health problems. My colleagues at Newnham made gradual, long-term contributions to my interpretations: Diana Lipton, Sheila Watts, Liz Watson, Jenny Mander, Pam Hirsch provided queries, comments, and criticisms that kept the project alive in the midst of other duties; Michael Payne never let me forget that fathers deserve to have their say about teenage daughters, and Ian Du Quesnay presented a strong argument against the assumption that paternal understatement implies lack of paternal passion.

Finally, I thank my own daughters, Miranda and Julia, who never give up on their task of teaching their mother about this relationship, who are eager to articulate what she does not know, and who are living proof that the hard work of mothering adolescent daughters is good work.

*You Don't Really Know Me*

# Love, Conflict, and Growth

**"THERE'S NO POINT** trying to explain.

"You won't understand.

"You don't know me.

"You don't have a clue who I really am."

A teenage girl spits these words through her tears and slams the door. The mother is hurt and outraged: How can her daughter say such things? Not know her! She's known her since the day she was born. She learned to read her feelings from the tiniest movements of her face and body. She interpreted her early half-formed words. She grew expert at identifying, and then anticipating her daughter's wishes and needs. Who dares now to cast that rich history aside? Where is the love that they both, so recently, took for granted?

What an ungrateful, spiteful daughter she has!

At the same time, she knows her daughter has a good heart, and she asks herself: "What have I done wrong? What have I done to make my daughter hate me?"

The woman's best friend, to whom she confides, explains: "It's not you. It's just a phase. She's being a typical teenager."

This reminder is reassuring, but only temporarily. Day to

day, face-to-face, her daughter speaks to her a strange language. Whatever teen tribe her daughter now belongs to, her
mother longs to understand the particular meanings this
particular girl utters, but her attempts at interpretation are
met with sneers.

Nothing shakes a woman's confidence in her mothering
skills as does the onset of her children's—and in particular
her daughter's—adolescence. The love that once was
bedrock now seems fragile. The communication that once
flowed easily, with words, glances, and touch, now is
diverted through rough channels. The aim of this book is to
chart this difficult terrain, so that mothers can follow the
changes in a daughter's needs and responses.

## The Long Road to Understanding

My first lesson in mothers' dread of a daughter's adolescence
came long before I became a teenager. My mother was
brooding over the fate of a neighborhood girl who, in her
view, was "heading for trouble" and her mother "couldn't do
anything about it."

"Doesn't her mother tell her what to do?" I asked, confident that maternal wisdom would set her right. "She's a
teenager," my mother replied. In response to my blank look,
she explained, "When you're a teenager you won't listen to a
word I say."

The world beyond my mother's convictions was a world
without intelligence or meaning, and she was telling me that
one day I would actually choose to dwell there. Aghast at the
vision of this catastrophic and unprotected landscape, I
demanded: "When will I be a teenager?"

She raised her chin thoughtfully to look at some future

which seemed to be residing just above my eye level. "When you're fourteen," she concluded crisply.

"Won't you still tell me things?" I pleaded.

"Oh, I'll try," she replied, "but you won't listen."

She was right, of course, in her fashion. Her version of our quarrels was that I didn't listen to anything she said. In her view, I was swallowed up by the calls of adolescence. I lost a child's concentration on a mother's rules and values. I lapsed into a world of my own enthusiasms and insecurities. I liked my music more than hers. I cared about hair more than homework. I remembered every detail of my girl-friend's new outfit but nothing of the shopping list she had entrusted to me.

In her view, I was following the typical teenage syndrome by rejecting her standards, rules, and wisdom. I was, in her view, endangering myself through my poor judgment. She saw me gripped by the power of my peers and hormones, and out of her control. Her fury was a measure of her fear.

While she saw me as a teenage rebel, I saw our battles in a different light. I longed for her recognition of a new me, of a person who sparkled with ability to set her own standards and mark her own goals. While my mother mourned the loss of her obedient child, I longed for her recognition of the new thoughts and aims that were engineering my development. Her prediction, "You won't listen to a word I say," became my complaint: "You don't listen to a word I say." So fright-ened was she of our differences that she saw only dangerous rebellion and was deaf to my pleas for recognition.

What, after all, did she want for me? Like most mothers, she wanted her daughter to be an independent person, self-motivated and self-directed. What did I want from her? I wanted to keep that significant bond between us, but to make room to develop according to my own lights. I wanted her to applaud this new development. In that sense I was, and would long remain, her very own daughter. So I continued to terrify her by my difference, even as I longed for her approval and pride.

When the battles subsided, her version was that she had won: I was no longer set against her because I was more grown-up. I could manage myself, both in day-to-day routines and in long-term planning. My version was that I had won: She acknowledged that I could think for myself, that I should be trusted to do what I wanted, and that, on the whole, she would be pleased by the results. Each of us kept our prejudice about the teenage conflict and resolution. Why reflect too much upon a war that was over?

It was when I had daughters of my own that my need to understand adolescence took on a new urgency. My nine-year-old daughter was helping me prepare for a day in the city. She chose the shirt to go with my suit. She checked my handbag, and commented on my hair. Having looked me over and decided I was ready to catch the train for my meeting, she said, "When I'm a teenager, I'll be able to go with you."

"Oh, when you're a teenager you won't want to go into the city with me," I predicted casually, treasuring the fleeting moments of her admiration. I saw the anticipation leave her face, which now wore a film of confused horror. "Why?" she demanded, tearful at this image of a future self with which she now had so little in common. And there it was, the old formula of teenage development, rolled up like a diploma my mother had handed me and which I was preparing to pass on to my daughter.

Psychological theories of adolescence have not changed

much in the course of these three generations. Teens are still monsters, hell-bent on rejecting their parents. It was at that moment I decided that the formula should be cast aside, that a new look at adolescence was necessary, and that I had my new project waiting, a gift my daughter gave me in exchange for the tired, destructive ideas I had tried to hand over to her.

## The Study

I began research on adolescent girls and their mothers in the mid 1980s. In 1990, *Altered Loves: Mothers and Daughters During Adolescence* was published, based on a series of interviews and observations of thirty-six mother/daughter pairs. This book was among the several publications that challenged the long-held assumption that rejection of parents was the key feature of adolescence.[1] Along with other researchers, I noted the importance of continuity and change in parent/child relationships. Girls, perhaps more markedly but not in total contrast to boys, put relationships in a central position, and developed within them. This counters the traditional theory that teenagers develop by separating from parents, but it does not explain why the bond comes under such tension during the teenage years.

The mother/daughter drama is constantly being played before our eyes, and yet its plot lines are difficult to see. During the past half century, it has generally been seen as a tussle between a girl's fight for freedom and a mother's urge to hold her back. Clinical reports of psychiatric patients frequently use the language of blame: Mothers are described as "engulfing," "controlling," "intrusive," "enmeshed," "seductive," "unempathic," "distant," or "depleted."[2] As Jane Smith, writing in the the *New York Times Magazine,* noted, "The indictment of mothers in the psychological literature has historically been so massive, so undifferentiated, and so oblivious of the actual limits of a mother's power or her context that it precludes a just assessment of real responsibility."[3]

Women are still given therapeutic "treatment" for a failure to separate from a mother. As clinicians see that girls and women are "incompletely separated" from a mother, they sometimes blame a mother's refusal to let go, and a mother's grudging fear that she will be abandoned or surpassed by an independent daughter. So deeply rooted is this theory in our culture that mother and adolescent daughter internalize the mandate to separate. As Janet Surrey writes, "Mothers are often very self-critical and blaming when they recognize their own desires for maintaining connection with their daughters, and often try to suppress or deny their own wishes. We need new models which allow us to validate relational yearning and strengths as well as difficulties in connections."[4]

This bias has led to distorted interpretations of teens' behavior. A teen's conflict with a mother is generally seen as a sign that she wants to separate. This myth has become so widespread that many parents use this framework as they interpret a daughter's day-to-day behavior. This interpretation influences a parent's response.

Linda, mother of fourteen-year-old Amy, says, "I know I have to let her go. I can feel myself holding on. It's a problem I have to work on, for her sake."

And Megan, mother of thirteen-year-old Sasha says, "I know what all this lip is about. She has to push me away. But knowing that doesn't help."

In recent years, however, there has been an exciting and radical shift in perspective whereby growth and development are measured through responsiveness, empathy, and connection, as much as through the old markers of independence and autonomy. But the shift in psychology that honors the importance of connection in girls' development has not put the poor mother/daughter press notices to rest. Even new research that reminds us of the importance of relationships in development casts suspicion on a mother's attachment. Mothers are described as using their influence to cut a daughter into shape. Believing that their daughters, as women, have to thrive in a culture that demands compliance and subservience from women, mothers are accused of forcing their daughters to conform to these standards. Our culture betrays women, and mothers, it is argued, to be good mothers, must betray their daughters; they must silence or suppress their inborn capacity for pleasure, observation, and full engagement with their environment.[5] So, while there has been a liberating shift in our view of girls' development, even the most recent accounts of the mother/daughter relationship ignore that lightning rod carrying empathy, understanding, and growth from one to the other.

## Putting the Two Halves Together

The stalemate of our understanding is enforced by a tendency to hear only half a story. The half story focuses on the ways girls and women often speak of their mothers. Sit a girl or woman down and ask her about her mother, and you will hear a string of complaints and criticisms. The other untold half of this story involves girls or women interacting with their mothers. Watch someone in action with her mother, ask her about an argument that ended five minutes ago, and you will hear something very different.

Studies based on the broader picture of mothers and daughters in a relational context give rise to a very different story. Complaints turn out to be superficial, or one strand of a complex braid. Criticisms tend to be ongoing conversations, signaling hope that understanding and resolution are around the corner. Within this relationship teenage girls learn to speak up and defend their own desires and their own views. Whereas outside the home girls may still be pressured to be nice, and still may pursue ideals of the perfect girl everyone likes, with a mother they seem to have a cultural sanction to speak out, talk back, give "lip." Conflict with a mother rarely puts the relationship at risk. Through conflict, mother and daughter often increase their understanding of each other, and remain close.

So the mother/daughter story has two sides. Even though I have been through the wringer of mothering two adolescent girls, I might, as a researcher, have failed to put these two sides together if I had listened only to teenage girls talk about their mothers, away from the dynamic of the relationship itself.

My research focuses on mothers and daughters in action. I speak to each individually, and I observe them together, in the natural habitat of their homes and neighborhoods. I watch them talk and laugh and quarrel. I ask them to reflect on recent conversations and conflicts. I catch them both in the heat of the moment and in the relative degrees of cool reflection.

## The Mother/Daughter Lab

My research amounts to a microscopic look at a living relationship through two different lenses. The first lens focuses on mothers and daughters in conversation. I look at the words they use. I mark their physical movements, their breathing, their facial expressions, their tone of voice. How do they use looks to communicate with each other? Which remark makes one turn away in silence, and which stimulates another to raise her voice? And then what happens? Is the raised voice on a trajectory to a blazing quarrel, or does it subside? Why does one rather than the other occur?

The second lens focuses on mothers and daughters reflecting on their interactions, especially their conflicts. How do they describe what happened? How do they feel about what's been said? Do they regret the pain they've caused, or do they plot revenge? In what context do they themselves put a recent argument. Is it a ripple or a tidal wave? When the heated moment has cooled, does one see the other's point of view, or does each glare at the other in frozen opposition?

The results of my investigations challenge a common assumption that the daughter is hell-bent on destroying the relationship and the parent intent on preserving the comfortable status quo of a daughter's childhood. Instead, we can see that both mother and daughter take on a range of roles; the daughter is capable of intricate repair work, just as the mother sometimes undermines the relationship as she digs herself into a defensive position. What the research shows, above all, is that mother/daughter conflict can be a means to closeness and understanding.

The material used in this book comes from the series of studies I have conducted during the past two decades. The first, conducted between 1984 and 1988, involved thirty-six mother/daughter pairs. The second, conducted between 1997 and 2002, followed twenty-three girls and their mothers at six-month intervals, tracking their evolving relationship over a four-year period. The conversations and conflicts presented in this book are drawn from the fifty-nine mother/daughter pairs of the two studies. The mothers and daughters came from two countries, the United States and the United Kingdom, though their ethnic range is broader than that. They included four Hispanic mothers and daughters from southern California; three Anglo-Indian pairs, living in the United Kingdon; nine African-American, all living in the Washington, D.C., area; two Chinese-American pairs from northern California. Race and ethnicity, however, are increasingly difficult to define. Thirteen mother/daughter pairs were first-generation mixed race; two were adopted, with different-race parents.

Providing a class tag is often as difficult as providing an ethnic one. A girl whose mother worked as a pattern cutter in a shoe factory described herself as upper middle class because her nonresident father was a managing director for an Internet company, and because she herself was heading toward college. A girl whose family owned a small delicatessen labeled herself "working class," whereas her cousin, who worked part-time in the shop with her, was "middle class" because her father had put up the money for the family business. While family backgrounds differed in many ways, basic mother/daughter dynamics were shared across the board.

I know that the process of observation changes what is observed. Some mothers and some daughters dramatize themselves as they would play to a camera, enhancing what they needlessly fear would be a boring text. Some mothers and some daughters play down either their anger or their love as too raw for exposure. But in putting together the observations of mothers and daughters interacting, and the one-on-one interviews, the point and purpose of mother/daughter conflicts are clear. The mother/daughter battle is an attempt to join a dance, during which each gains a series of different views of the other, and each in the end can be the winner. Both mothers and daughters change as a result of their daily interactions, and they change each other. A girl's development takes place within a context over which she has a great deal of influence. Sometimes a mother is not a good partner in her daughter's development—but this is not the norm. Normally, a mother tries to improve her understanding of her daughter, to gain her daughter's confidence, and to use what she knows about her daughter to aid her growth.

The widespread tendency to misinterpret a daughter's moves can have an impact on the quality of the relationship. All too often, mothers interpret a daughter's aggression as a sign that she is trying to move away. Misinterpreting as signs of rejection a daughter's coded attempts at a new engagement with her, a mother may pull back, leaving a daughter emotionally alone and frustrated. Understanding the real meaning of a teenage daughter's words is the key to a strong, useful, and enduring relationship.

# 1. *The Mother/Daughter Plot*

**COMPLAINTS ABOUT MOTHERS** trip easily off the tongues of teenage girls. Among friends, they compete to lodge the most vehement protest about their "impossible mothers."

"My mother treats me like I'm still her little girl. She doesn't know a thing about me," Clara reports. Her words run together, the volume rises and falls like a piston, and she stares at me, daring me, as a representative of the adult world, to defend the person she is attacking. "You have no idea," she reminds me, "how infuriating that is."

Gina's hands are poised as claws on either side of her face and make pincer movements as she speaks. "I feel smothered by her. She wants to wrap me in a little cocoon and keep me away from the big bad world until I'm ready to die." She and Clara laugh. "When I'm old and shriveled and ready to die, I'll be safe," Gina adds.

The third fourteen-year-old in the group, Amanda, is not to be outdone. "My mother doesn't have a clue about how I feel about things. She has no idea how mad she can make me. Even when I'm screaming in her face, she doesn't get just how mad I am."

The three girls fall silent as the flush in Amanda's face rises, then gradually subsides. She chews her lips and the others wait for her to add something, but she just shrugs as though to say, "Why bother going on with this? Mothers are useless."

Above us we hear a phone ring, then footsteps, and the outlines of a voice. "Ooo—she's home." Gina flinches as her mother calls down into the basement rec room, "Clara's mom is on her way." Gina sticks out her tongue ("The sound of that woman's voice!"). Clara smiles understandingly, and gets up to leave.

The girls troop upstairs. "Hi, sweety," Roberta greets her daughter, who silently mimics, "Hi, sweety," with a staged smile and sideways shake of her head. Roberta notices this, bites her upper lip, and sighs. She then ignores Gina and turns to me for the reprieve of a polite and controlled exchange. Gina overtalks our conversation and slams the front door when her friends leave. The domestic air has the electrical charge of a brewing quarrel. Both mother and daughter are keen to begin.

"A little respect would be appreciated," Roberta informs Gina. After a pause, during which she decides not to pursue this, she begins, "It's Thursday. You're going swimming tonight. You've spent the entire afternoon with friends. I hope you've finished your homework."

"I'm not going swimming!"

"Check the schedule. And don't shout at me!"

"Don't shout at me!" Gina looks at the swimming schedule on the refrigerator door, makes a face, shrugs. "Shit! I really don't feel like swimming."

"Well, it's up to you. You're the one who signed up for this."

"I know! I just don't feel like going today. But I will. Okay? I know it's up to me."

"But I'm the one who has to drive you."

"Jees, Mom! Will you get off my back! I forgot. Okay? I'm really really sorry. Okay?"

"It's not just this. You forgot you were baby-sitting on Tuesday. You forgot to stop at the cleaners—."

"What is this? Some stupid, you know, some stupid—inquisition?"

"I'm just saying—. We talked about this before. We talked about responsibility—."

"I am responsible."

"You're not organized enough to be responsible. I'm just going over what we already discussed. When I have a lot to remember, I make a list, and look at it in the morning and—"

"I don't care what you do! I'm not you. Okay? You're driving me nuts. You're always judging me."

"I'm not judging you! I'm just concerned. I don't know what's with you."

"No, Mom, you don't. You don't even begin to know. There's no point in trying to tell you, because you really don't know." After a minute's silence, she adds, "I'll go swimming. Maybe Mandy's mom can take me."

"I'll take you."

"Let me ask Mandy!"

"I'll take you. I don't mind. We'll eat early."

"Do you want some help?"

"No, you do what homework you have to do—."

"I don't have much. I don't!" she insists when her mother looks at her.

"Okay. Does Mandy want a lift?"

"I'll ask her."

## Common Clashes

Mothers and daughters argue about many things. They argue about boyfriends and curfews, housework and homework. They argue about respect (and displays of disrespect), appreciation (or lack of it), willingness or resistance to understand each other and listen to what the other has to say. Arguments can flare up over food, hair, clothes, posture, tone of voice. They can begin with a premeditated scolding and prepackaged punishment, as a mother waits for the sound of the key in the door, filled with both relief and rage at her daughter's late return. They can descend out of the blue, in the midst of a carefree shopping expedition, as a mother's passing comment bursts open a criminal file a daughter has been keeping on her mother's assumptions and attitudes.

It isn't easy dealing with an angry daughter. Teens like to begin with *harsh start-ups* that tend to make the other person angry and defensive: "You are ruining my social life. No one wants to come to this house with all your stupid rules."

Everything becomes an issue of debate: "I wasn't an hour late. It was at most thirty minutes. You always exaggerate what I do," Or, "I wasn't drunk. I had maybe two drinks. I wasn't drunk. You don't know anything."

We respond on several levels. The first is practical: "How am I going to get my point across and maintain the control necessary to keep my teenager safe and preserve my household peace?"

There is also the response we have at an egoistic level: "What right does someone have to contradict me and criticize me?"

And there is the deep emotive level: "Does my daughter's anger mean she no longer loves me?"

Our range of responses can cloud our perception of what is going on and our judgment as to how to manage what's going on.

## An Intimate History

Children quickly pick up and follow the nuances and rhythms of human connection. Early in their lives, they focus on their mother's responses. Infants, once considered by psychologists to be incapable of relating to another person, have now been discovered to initiate connection, respond to others, and remember the moves that elicited responses. Films of mother and baby catch these two people in the acts of finding and losing their engagement, moving in and out of touch, turning away and turning to each other.[1]

In adolescence, these rhythms of relationship between mother and daughter still occur, but they change. Both mothers and daughters have difficulty keeping this relationship current. A mother holds close the memories of a child as an infant, and throughout her life she will continue to see (and also evoke!) the child in her daughter. In a mother's eyes, the daughter is not one child but several much-loved children, all evolving within a changing body. While a teenager has a vehement (and uncertain) opinion of who she is now, a mother may be responding to the child ten years, ten months, or ten days before—and hence get things very wrong.

A daughter's efforts to update the mother, and her impatience with someone who can be an infuriatingly slow learner, give rise to irritation on the daughter's part and bewilderment on the mother's part. The need both mother and daughter feel to maintain and renegotiate the relationship, in the midst of these changes, is the crux of mother/daughter conflict during the daughter's teenage years.

## Making Sense of Teen Battles

More tension arises between an adolescent daughter and her mother than between any other parent/child pair. On average, there is an identifiable conflict (let's call it a fight or argument or quarrel) between mother and teenage daughter every two and half days, whereas there is, on average, a four-day reprieve between mother/son fights. Arguments between mothers and daughters tend to last about fifteen minutes, compared to mothers' arguments with sons, which tend to last about six minutes.[2]

At the same time, most teenage girls describe the relationship with a mother as "close" and "supportive" and, above all, they say it is "important." They want to engage a mother in a vital way, and sometimes they do this by provoking conflict. Their aim is to make authentic contact. Mothers sometimes back away from this intense engagement—usually because they have learned to interpret the fights as a sign that a daughter wants to separate from them. They then do not understand the positive aim of this apparently negative contact.

The vast majority of teenagers like their parents, share their values, and seek a good relationship with them. In general, they describe their family relationships in positive terms, emphasizing the supportive and emotionally meaningful nature of their lives together. Generally speaking, our

ɔ not hate us, however angry they may be with us.
ɡenerally speaking, our teens want a good, close rela-
ʃhip with us.

Mother/daughter arguments are characterised by an
exquisite attentiveness to each other's views and emotions.
Their quarrels occur within a strongly bonded relationship,
in which each looks to the other for love and recognition, in
which each has learned to have high expectations of the
other. The tension that characterizes a mother/teenage
daughter bond not only emerges from love, but also regulates it.

## Why do Mothers and Daughters Have Such a Passionate Relationship?

Why do teenage girls have such an intense relationship with
their mothers? Why do they display powerful feelings of
both love and resentment?

All parent/child bonds gain a special potency through
their basic connections to the deepest aspects of life: birth,
growth, care, loss, death. Fathers and sons, in very different ways, have high expectations of each other, and of the
bond between them, but they negotiate their love by less
direct means. Mothers and sons share an intense love for
each other, but this intensity tends to be regulated in childhood, as a boy's gender education informs him of the significant differences between him and his mother. By the
time a boy reaches adolescence, he probably loves his
mother as much as his sister does, but without the mag-
netism of identification.

Girls reach adolescence with a deep psychological identification with their mothers. A teenage girl is becoming a

woman, like her mother; but how similar she will be, and how different she may want to be, are questions that shape, day to day, both the broad and immediate themes of her life. They influence her choice of friends and her future plans. They are considerations in her assessment of hairstyles and clothes and jewelry, defining her as like or not like mother's ideal for her.

However drastically this bond changes as a girl moves into adolescence, it persists. Girls do not construct an identity, as boys are thought to do, by marking personal boundaries between themselves and their mothers at a very early age. While it is an overstatement to say boys "separate" from their mothers in early childhood, they do generally develop with a clear knowledge that they are different sorts of people, and different in a very basic way, from the parent who is most likely to be their primary parent. Girls tend to retain a close relationship with a mother throughout childhood, and a comfortable identification (I look to her for who I'll be/I want to be a lot like her/I am a lot like her). Consequently, in adolescence, there is an urge to exaggerate her differences from her mother. A daughter harbors an uneasy sense that these differences have to be earned and proved and guarded. "I'm nothing like my mother" is a remark a teenage girl will make as a political platform; it is a stand to be defended, rather than a simple statement of fact.

Sometimes she fights her mother to clarify her difference to herself, and sometimes her mother experiences this as rejection. "I don't want to be just like you" can, in the heat of those many confused moments, become "I don't like you at all." Most women look back on their teenage years as a time when an intense relationship with a mother, both positive and negative, shaped awareness of who she was (and wasn't), and of who she wanted to be, and who she did not want to become. But, as we see our daughter whipped by negative feelings, the perspective we have gained by traveling some distance from our own adolescence is often lost.

A teenage daughter maintains a critical watchfulness over her own identity, and locates herself carefully by being "not my mother." This underlies the irritation girls frequently express when a mother points out similarities. "I know just how you feel," or "I went through the same thing when I was your age" are often said to offer comfort; but a teenage daughter believes "You do not know how I feel," or "It's not the same thing you went through," or "How do you know?" These are the challenges mothers meet when they take the steps that usually work to show sympathy and understanding.

Much has been said about women's conversational styles as a means of negotiating closeness,[3] but the mother/daughter conversational dance differs from ordinary woman-talk. Girls tend to confide in a mother to underline their uniqueness and hence their difference from a mother, not their commonality and similarity.

But the mother/daughter identification, based on parent/child closeness and deepened by sharing a gender, is not a one-way process. Mothers do see themselves in a daughter, and much of a daughter's battle with the mother is against this identification. "I'm not like you," "I'm not yours," "My body doesn't belong to you" are sometimes necessary reminders.

"I know I'm not you!" we say, our outrage and defense tripping quickly from our tongue. But while we look starkly at the ways in which we know a daughter is not us and that her life belongs to her, she spots our half-formed expectations and assumptions that we may not notice. To improve our responsiveness to a daughter, to give her what she needs to grow, to be a light in front of her (as well as a shadow from behind), we have to endure the grueling process of listening to the truth of her horrendous accusations. If the ideal of similarity is something a mother craves, if she feels that the daughter, in denying that she is like her, is rejecting her, then the confidences may stop. So too do the quarrels. But absence of conflict is very different from a good relationship.

## A Typical Spat

The tiff between Gina and her mother, Roberta, is a typical blip in a teenage daughter's and mother's day. Gina strengthens her bond with her girlfriends by swapping complaints about their impossible mothers. When her mother suddenly enters her world, she is irritated, and feels honor bound to express this irritation in front of her friends. This makes Roberta angry, and as soon as the other girls leave, Roberta reminds her daughter she would like to be treated with respect.

From Roberta's point of view, this is a reasonable request, and a mild response to the disrespect her daughter displays in front of others, but it is a red flag to a teen. Roberta adds to the maternal weight by reminding Gina of her swimming schedule, her homework, her overall level of responsibility. While she tries to frame her reminder in terms of Gina's independent choices ("You're the one who signed up for this"), Gina feels cornered. She hates being told the decision is up to her: She claims she knows this, but her mother's reminder implies the opposite. Then her mother says that her decision affects her too ("But I'm the one who has to drive you") which Gina shouts down, ("Will you get off my back"), but follows with an apology, albeit a cold formulaic one ("I'm really really sorry. Okay?")

Roberta does not allow this bristling apology to close the matter. She places the specific issue in a wider context: Gina has forgotten several commitments over the past weeks. When Gina rejects this list of omissions, Roberta emphasizes her point with the general remark about Gina's responsibility. Gina defends herself by attacking her mother for being judgmental, and then challenges her capacity to judge anything she does ("You really don't know").

Teens may be impulsive and disorganized, but they are acute observers and adept arguers. They demand clarity and have high standards of consistency for parents who set down rules and conditions; that is one reason arguing with them can be so frustrating. Gina notes every wayward move in Roberta's argument. She sees that when her mother says, "It's up to you," she is really telling her what she should do. She refuses to let her mother get away with labeling her "irresponsible," and she deftly twists away from her mother's attempt to give her advice in the form "This is what I do/This is what you should do." Roberta tries to be reasonable and keep to the point, but, like most mothers, she is no match for her argumentative daughter, who refuses to accept the frame of the argument as one of a mother instructing her daughter (how to be respectful, how to be organized, how to be responsible). Instead, Gina frames it in terms of who can judge whom, and whether her mother is in a position to know her at all.

What is perhaps most remarkable is the way Gina then moves to close the argument with an agreement to go swimming. Roberta accepts this with an offer to drive her. Mother and daughter then begin a gentle competition as to who can be most considerate of the other: Gina will see if Amanda's mother will do the driving; Roberta suggests that Gina finish her homework rather than help prepare dinner. A new argument threatens to brew (will her mother challenge what Gina says about the amount of homework she has?) but then subsides as Roberta makes a decision to accept her daughter's word.

## Strategies That Can Be Counterproductive

Quarrels like this one can offer both mother and daughter a sense of being active in the relationship. Each proves her capacity for responding effectively. Each impacts on the other, each moves the relationship toward authentic connection, and each is able to be moved and receptive.

Arguments seldom destroy a mother/daughter relationship. The most important lesson I have learned from my years of research on parents and teens is that it is not the number of quarrels a parent and teenager have that destroys a relationship, but what happens during some quarrels.

What can destroy this relationship are strategies that parents sometimes use to control an angry teen, or to protect their own status as parents. Most parents, tempted to employ these strategies, then yield to a daughter's response, thereby allowing her to influence the outcome. But anger and outrage and fear can make us cling to these strategies, which arouse irritation, anger, or a sense of insult in a daughter. These strategies are not necessarily to be avoided at all times, but should be recognized for what they are: moves in an argument that will lead to countermoves by a daughter.

The most common of these strategies include:

*Laying Down the Law*

Parents pull out all stops to regain authority when they see they are losing control, but teens don't like being told what to do, or "ordered around."

*Criticism*

At the top of teens's hate list is "being judged."

*Ridicule*

Teens don't like being mocked, made fun of, or humiliated.

*Silencing*

This can range from ignoring what's being said to punishing a girl who speaks out. Teens complain bitterly about not being listened to, being ignored, or being told, by whatever means, to shut up.

Understanding the point and purpose of arguments does not ensure that we will avoid destructive moves, but it helps us avoid taking such steps blindly. Understanding can temper our self-righteousness. After all, arguing with parents is a legitimate teenage activity. It is a means of making sure one is heard. It is a means of rejecting restrictions and renegotiating family rules. It is a means of modifying expectations and correcting assumptions. It is an attempt to make one's new grown-up space within the familiar family bonds.

## Healthy Fighting

Fighting well with a mother is an important skill. "She challenges everything I say," Roberta reflects. In fact, Gina is learning how to negotiate authority, deflect criticism, and stand up for herself.

Fighting well with a mother encourages a girl to develop skills to manage conflict with other girls and women. Some years ago, the psychotherapists Luise Eichenbach and Susie Orbach noted the terror some women experience in conflict with other women, either as friends or colleagues. They argued convincingly that the hidden aggression in girls and women[4] goes back to a fear of conflict and competition with a mother.[5] They found that the women who were particularly anxious about disagreements with other women habor the fantasy that open conflict with a mother would result in abandonment.

These fears can be addressed during the adolescent years. Girls can learn that arguing with their mothers does not bring them to the brink of disaster. They can learn that jostling for status with a mother is a legitimate activity, and that therefore they are not going to destroy a valued relationship if they resist another woman's attempt to pull rank. The competence and confidence they acquire through their passionate relationship with a mother prepare them for the interpersonal tasks of life.

## How Does Understanding Help?

To say something innocent and friendly, and find you have caused offense; to try to be helpful and be thought interfering; to show affection and be told you are making a nuisance of yourself; to offer praise and be told you're incapable of judgment; to give advice and be attacked like an enemy: These are the glitches that can undermine one's sense of competence and value. Mothering a teenage daughter is not easy.

Having studied mothers and adolescent daughters for nearly twenty years, I am convinced that understanding is the key to change. A mother who understands the positive purpose of inevitable quarrels with her daughter can help make sense of the tension and exhaustion they engender. A shift in perception will transform a quarrel from a defeat into an opportunity. Negotiation—of rules, of status, of values—will become a useful parenting task, rather than drudgery. It will be seen as a contribution to the meaning and quality of a mother's relationship with her daughter. Instead of seeing control as the means of safety, she will see acknowledgment as the way forward. Instead of feeling that a quarrel signals maternal redundancy, she will understand that it is a signal of her daughter's continuing need.

Mothers sometimes experience a crisis of confidence when a daughter goes through adolescence because the tactics that worked so well when the daughter was a child no longer work. A mother who could comfort her moody or weepy ten-year-old may find that her efforts to comfort her fourteen-year old are counterproductive. Instead of comforting her, she increases her irritation.

If a mother concludes that her daughter does not want her anymore, or doesn't need her, she feels useless.

A change in perspective in which she sees that her daughter still needs her would inspire her to keep trying, to find new ways of offering comfort and understanding.

Many quarrels escalate because the mother feels rejected and hurt. Once these quarrels are understood, it will be easier to withstand the ego blows that go with parenting a teenager. Our daughters teach us that we are imperfect, and clumsy in our love. They also teach us how to improve, and remind us that our responses are always important to them. This book does not provide a blueprint for solutions to mother/daughter problems. It presents relationships as works in progress. It offers a new explanation as to the purpose of conflict and the meanings of quarrels. It underlines the abiding dilemma of maternal protectiveness as it confronts two imperatives: to keep a daughter safe, and to foster her growth. It offers a new understanding to incorporate facts, old half-truths, new half-truths.

The facts are:

- Mothers and teenage daughters fight more than any other parent/child pair.
- A daughter's relationship with her mother has a lifelong impact on her sense of self and well-being.

Some pervasive, destructive mother/daughter myths are:

- Teenage girls want to separate from their mothers, both psychologically and emotionally.
- Teen conflict with a parent is an attempt to cut off emotional and psychological bonds.
- Rebellious behavior and conflict go hand in hand, and are part of the same urge to disconnect from a parent.
- To the extent that teenage girls are unable to separate from a mother, their growth stagnates.
- Mothers are afraid of being abandoned by their daughters and so give mixed messages about independence and growth.
- Mothers, having themselves been frustrated in their own personal goals, are envious of daughters with more opportunities.
- Girls take one step forward and away, only to be filled

with fear that they will destroy or punish a mother by moving on.

- Teenage girls undergo a progressive self-silencing process, and mothers usually participate in this process.

New understanding confirms that:

- Mother/daughter arguments are a process whose aim is to negotiate a daughter's identity.
- Teenage girls seek a new balance rather than distance or separation from a mother.
- The aim of conflict with mother and daughter is to change the relationship and to move close on different terms.
- Far from colluding in attempts to silence teenage girls, mothers liberate a girl's articulate self-awareness.

# 2.

# *"You're not listening!":*
# *The Battle for Recognition*

OUR RESPONSES to people we love have a deep and complex history, and this history guides our interpretation of what it is they are doing. The psychological and emotional intimacy of mothers and daughters means that these histories impact on even the most minor interchanges, particularly during adolescence when the question of identity looms so large. For at this time, the various guises of that question, "Who am I?" color this relationship. If mothers learn to place a daughter's criticisms and complaints in this context, they can use them to strengthen the relationship.

When teenage girls complain about their mothers, they frequently complain about how their mothers see them:

"She sees me as her little girl."

"She sees me as a slut."

"She thinks I'm Miss Goody-Two-Shoes."

"In her view I'm lazy and superficial."

"The way she sees things, I'm not going to amount to anything."

Or,

"She can't see how much this matters to me."

"She can't see that I have to make my own decision."
And then:

"She thinks she knows me better than I know myself."

"She thinks she knows what's best for me."

"It's that smugness—like she knows the truth and I know zilch—that really gets me going."

Unprepared for these complaints and unaware of the needs that underlie them, mothers say: "The minute I open my mouth, she complains." "I can't say anything without her jumping on me. I don't know what she wants. I'm better off keeping my mouth shut."

What *do* teenage girls want from their mothers?

In fact, they do not want a mother who leaves them alone and does not speak. They want connection, recognition, and respect.

## Connection

When I began research on mothers and daughters about twenty years ago, my questions were framed by the then-current assumption that the "task" of adolescence was separation from the parent. At that time, developmental theory followed Anna Freud's model of adolescence as a parent/child version of divorce.[1] Adolescent development was seen as a process during which a teen casts off her early love and idealization of her parents and, turning away from them, embraces friends and media icons who, in her eyes, have the glamour, strength, and wisdom that she once saw in her now-redundant parents.

I then set out to understand how teenage girls "succeed" or "fail" to separate from the person to whom they have (most probably) been closest throughout infancy and childhood. In line with current theory, I expected mother/daughter quarrels to signal a girl's effort to snap childhood bonds of love and attachment.

After listening to girls describing their relationships to mothers, and, above all, watching the dynamic interplay of mother and daughter, I realized that my questions were coming from the wrong direction. Rather than asking how daughters become independent and separate, it is more to the point to ask how daughters retain their attachment to their mothers as they themselves grow and change. The "task" of adolescence is not to sever the closeness, but to alter it.

The issues at stake when daughters initiate quarrels with a mother are "How do I get her to see who I really am?" and "How can I make her understand me and appreciate me as I am now?" and "How can I get her to see I'm no longer the child I used to be?" Above all, the issue is "How can I keep this important relationship up-to-date and useful to me?"

But, if teenage girls value connection with a mother, why do they give her such a hard time?

Teens criticize and contradict their parents. They bristle when parents speak. In fact, they acquire the attitudinal equivalent of porcupine spines that rise like a prickly shield when parents set down rules, offer advice, or even when they offer affection and comfort. In addition, teens want to do their own thing and go their own way, free from parental control. They want to set their own life pace and adopt their own lifestyle. All this appears consistent with a wish to reject a parent.

But this process of "individuation"—a growing awareness of oneself as distinct from one's parents—should not be confused with psychological separation.[2] The terms *individua-*

*tion* and *separation* appear together so frequently in psychological theory that their different meanings are often blurred.

Individuation involves the development of a more or less distinct self, someone who can distinguish her own wishes, hopes, and needs from those of others, especially those close to her, such as a parent. Individuation is always a matter of degree. It shifts throughout our lives. One's identification of oneself and sense of self-boundaries are constantly shifting. A toddler parades her discovery that what she wants at that moment is something very different from what her parent wants. A toddler wants to leave the store, but her mother stays. She wants her sandwich cut in a certain way, but her mother cuts it differently. So confusing and terrifying is this difference that she screams with rage. Her tantrum, which can seem like defiance, is also an expression of fear and confusion.

A somewhat older child may be able to identify her own preferences, but may be unable to distinguish her values from those of a parent. She knows she wants things that her mother denies her, but she may not yet realize that she can have different ideas about important things, such as religion, politics, and day-to-day values.

As a teen, however, she realizes, "My mother thinks this, but I don't." She may try to hammer her differences out by adopting opposing views and values, carefully chosen, always with an eye on a parent's response. "See, I can now think for myself," she implicitly declares. As an adult, she may continue to refine her differences. "That's not what I want, really. I only thought I wanted it because I thought it would please my mother."

This sense of who we are, what we want, and what we

value, as opposed to what others want or expect from us, is never fixed and final. We experience ourselves in different ways with different people. Those to whom we are close, especially, define and create new aspects of ourselves. A sideways look or an offhand remark can remind us of something we have forgotten; it can make us feel whole and strong, or it can uncover awful feelings, and mark out depression or shame. This is part of what it means to be human, that we form our sense of self in an intimately interpersonal world.

Separation is used in psychological theories to denote a clearly bounded self, one not interlocked with anyone else. "Standing on one's own two feet" and "knowing one's own mind" are phrases that indicate some of the meanings of separation in this sense of the term. Here, a maturing person is expected to cut those internal ties with others (especially with a mother). Where separation is seen as a key to psychological development, a mature person would know precisely where her wishes and aims and needs ended, and those of another person began. She would know herself fully in the absence of others, or even in the absence of any relationship with others, and she would feel herself to be the same person with different people.

But being individual and constructing oneself in relation to other people are complementary, not contradictory, processes. Most teenagers are eager to discover who they really are and to find what they would call their own way in life, but they discover their own way through interactions with others and, most of all, through interactions with a mother. This is a difficult process for a teen. She makes sure it is difficult for her mother, too.

## Mirroring

We all feel uncomfortable when we are ignored, or when we feel someone doesn't see us for who we are. But a child's need for a parent's recognition has a special urgency and a long history.

A child is born into a relationship with a parent, and immediately joins a complex and changing interplay of sounds, touch, and looks. As the infant grows, she becomes physically independent, able to move away from those upon whom she has been utterly dependent. She discovers the meaning of her actions and the value of her skills, in part, through her own experience, but also with reference to her mother's face and voice.

As she exercises her limbs, and in many other ways discovers her ability to move and act at will, she is encouraged by a parent's approval and quailed by her anxiety. She races toward the swings and turns to meet the mother's amazement at her skill. She cries out in distress, long before she falls, as she sees fear on her parent's face.

The process of looking to a parent for approval of one's developing skills and acts of will is called "mirroring." In other words, the child looks into a parent's face to read the meaning of what she herself is doing.

Mirroring has been identified as an important process of growth in the early phase of childhood when a child begins her journey of physical independence from the adults who care for her.[3] "Is it safe to move away?" "Will I be able to find my way back?" "Is it acceptable to act on my own?" "If I make use of my independence, will I be able to return to the familiar safe haven upon which I still depend?" These are questions that fashion a two- and three-year-old's first excursions.

Though mirroring, in this form, has a special psychological force in early childhood, it retains its importance throughout childhood and adolescence—and beyond. Few adolescents do not care what a parent thinks of them, and few do not watch a parent carefully, trying to read a parent's responses: "Is it okay if I do this?" "Do you mind if I do that?" Arguments about control are not only about rules; they are also about feelings. "Am I allowed to do this?" is a minor question compared to the searching query "Are you okay with my doing this?" Teens assess the response to this query, and continually work to shape it. The answers they read from a parent's responses probably will not stop them from doing what they want to do, but will influence how they feel about it.

A teenager, characteristically and predictably, tries to shake the parent into a recognition and appreciation of her newly emerging self. She asks for recognition of a self that is barely formed. She sees enormous changes, whereas parents see the child they have known all along. She fights for this recognition not because she is obstreperous or vain, but because she cannot formulate her own sense of self in isolation from a parent's recognition. Learning about oneself and constructing oneself are at one with these strong and abiding relationships. Teenagers develop a sense of who they are through their relationship with a parent. In particular, a girl turns to her mother.

## Respect

Complaints about disrespect, and remarks about the importance of respect, are common in any discussion of the mother/daughter relationship. But what counts as respect?

In the context of mother and teenage daughter, respect is closely linked to recognition.

Teenage girls turn to their mothers for self-confirmation. A daughter plots and plans to find some means of wresting acknowledgment from a mother. If necessary, she will shock her mother into submission. Some girls behave outrageously to get any response that is different from those responses her mother would have bestowed on her as a child. This is different from simple attention seeking. A daughter is not petulantly insisting, as a child might, that her mother "pay attention." She is seeking a measured response that will change the blueprint held in her mother's mind.

Until she is able to find a regular and reliable route to detailed communication, she will do just about anything to disturb her mother's complacency about "my daughter" or "my little girl" or "the child I know." Interchanges between mother and teenage daughter are full of identity reminders: "I can take care of myself," "I'm not stupid, you know," "I know what I'm doing," "You can't tell me what to do." Girls tend to be touchy and sharp-witted with a mother who assumes she knows just how her daughter feels. In a teen's view, respect is acknowledgment of her brand-new self.

A teen insists that her mother does not understand her—does not even know her—because her mother may think she knows this girl well, or because her mother is not amazed or terrified by the bright new self the daughter herself cannot quite believe in, which is there but just beyond her line of vision. She is touchy, sulky, critical as she seeks her mother's hand in this partnership of growth. It is not surprising that her bizarrely expressed aims are so often misunderstood.

In spite of all her bravado, she feels unformed and

unproven. While she presents confidence to her mother, she harbors a myriad of doubts herself. Behind her proud stance is a keen awareness of how easily she can be exposed or shamed or ridiculed. In self-protection, many teens develop romantic notions about an emerging self— that it is unique, unknown, misunderstood, that its truth can be revealed only through secret rites of diary confessions or protected confidences among friends.[4] Her ability to express who she is always seems somehow to fall short of who she feels she is or is about to become—and she often blames this shortfall on her mother's inadequate understanding.

### You Never Listen to a Word I Say!

When a teenage girl believes that her mother does not recognize or respect her, she generally expresses this by saying that her mother does not listen to her. The teen knows that her parent literally hears her words. Her mother may respond and reply, but not in a way that shows understanding and acceptance, and not in a way that allows what a daughter says to influence what her mother thinks.

The accusation of not listening is, in the interpersonal arena, a serious one. No one likes not being heard. But not listening can take many forms. There's the obvious one of simply not responding to a person, refusing or neglecting to talk to someone, not noticing, or pretending not to notice someone who's in the room. Other forms of not listening are less obvious, but just as enraging and confusing. Not listening, in the sense of not taking in what's said, can frustrate a teen who grows through her mother's acknowledgment.

Without that, she feels shut in a vacuum. However fierce her bid to be her own person, and different from her mother, she negotiates her development with an eye on her mother's responses.

Daughters use their mothers as a sounding board for their thoughts, their ideas, and their emerging persona. For many reasons, a girl feels that her sense of self is bound up with her mother. She seeks independence, but she needs a mother to acknowledge the new person she is becoming. Does her mother understand just how different she is now, from the child she was? Does her mother appreciate how deeply she now thinks about things? Does she acknowledge the legitimacy of her daughter's perspective? Does she appreciate the value of her daughter's experiences?

Conversations with a mother can go awry as a girl explains something and then gets a response she considers out-of-date. Sasha tells her mother about a problem at school, which is also partly a friend problem. "Kirsty was acting like she owns the place, and she said there were already too many people signed up [to work on a mural for the gym]." But when her mother, Megan, says, "That's too bad. I'm sorry," Sasha shouts, "That's not what I mean. You're not listening!" She wants to tell her mother about her disappointment, but she also wants to feel that she is managing the situation. Her mother's sympathy strikes a sour chord, which her mother cannot hear, and which Sasha herself might have great difficulty identifying. Feeling both misunderstood and unable to explain, she gets angry. Quarreling can be a way of making sure that someone works harder to hear what you are trying to say.

## Can We Talk?

Adolescent daughters rate "talking" as the thing they like doing most with their mothers. However selective they are about what they tell her, they are quick to assess her responses to what they do reveal. While daughters enjoy talking with their mothers, they also criticize the process. They complain that a mother isn't sufficiently pleased or upset by a piece of news. She doesn't seem adequately engaged with a daughter's problem. She just doesn't get it. She asks one question too many. She's annoying. She's interfering. She says "the wrong thing" because she "isn't really listening."

Teens are right: We often don't listen. While we are basically interested in them, habit, and the distractions of our own daily lives, can take over our responses. We nod automatically as they chatter like children, while we search for our briefcase, compose a shopping list, prepare the dinner. "Did you really?" "That's nice," and then "Mmmhmm." Or, we may say in response to something that rings out of tune with what we expect, "You don't mean that."

"You don't listen" is a charge we hotly deny: We want to get to know this person to whom we are so attached; and yet listening is hard. When all a mother may want is a simple break, a moment's peace, a daughter demands her full attention. To listen to someone, not only do we have to pay attention to what's being said; we also have to challenge our assumptions about who our daughter is and what she feels.

In this context, "not listening" has a broad meaning. We fail to listen when we say, "You shouldn't feel that way," or "You shouldn't say that." We fail to listen when we tell a daughter that things aren't as she sees them, or that she is not in a position to speak her own mind because she's "too young to judge" or "too hot headed to understand." We fail to listen when we tell her to keep her mouth shut, or not to talk like that, or demand, "How dare you say such a thing?" A girl also feels silenced by a mother who feels so anxious when certain issues are raised that she fidgets, changes the subject, or denies what she hears. "You don't mean that" or "You're not serious" or "I don't believe you" are among the many versions of silencing a daughter.

Learning anew to listen to what a teenage daughter says is different from agreeing with what she says. Our listening provides what Lyn Mikel Brown calls self-authorization—an ability to know and claim the rightness of one's feelings and thoughts, even in the face of disagreement, disappointment, and anger.[5] When we listen, we give a daughter permission to say what she thinks, sees, knows, and feels. In addition, we can listen by amplifying what she says; we draw a daughter's voice out, help her go further in what she wants to say, encourage her to find the words that express her thoughts and feelings.

While most mothers intuitively follow good listening practice most of the time, their daughters remain critical of them, and focus on the times they fail to listen. Arguments about the quality of a mother's response are the most common of all types of mother/daughter argument. It is not the specific content of a mother's words, but their implications as to her position vis-à-vis her daughter that ignite rage. "Don't keep telling me what to do," or "Stop trying to run my life for me," or "Back off!" are familiar countermoves against parental authority. The complaints behind these are: "You don't see/appreciate/understand that I can take care of myself."

And while parent-to-teen admonishment of manner and voice ("Don't use that tone of voice with me") is understandable, necessary, and common, less well recognized, but equally common, are complaints a daughter has about a mother's attitude or tone of voice. These are often unrecognized because a teen's rage is not always articulate—partly because her anger is way out of proportion to the situation. She may grunt and stomp out of the room, or utter a global complaint ("You are so annoying"), or exclaim "Mo-ther" or "Mo-om" in elongated syllables that map out the depths of her despair. In a daughter's eyes, the mother is hopeless. In a mother's eyes, the daughter is totally unreasonable. Both viewpoints are understandable. If each understood the other, the quarrels would be productive.

Daughters are harsh critics of mothers' responses because they have high expectations. A mother can enrage her daughter with a simple word or gesture that fails to shape the right response. A daughter may accuse a mother of total lack of interest or understanding if she has a momentary loss of concentration, or changes the subject, or offers a sigh ("Not this again"). Mere humans do not have an easy time when they are mothers of teenage daughters.

## *"You don't know who I am!"*

Amy admits that her mother "isn't a bad mother. But I turn into this stupid person when I'm with her, because she keeps getting me all wrong."

Girls want their mothers to work at getting to know them, to listen even when they whisper. They want their mothers to get to know them and then to love them for themselves. Amy complains, "She loves me because I'm her daughter. She doesn't see who I really am. It doesn't mean anything if you love a person but don't know them."

Amy, at fifteen, wants her mother to follow her development. Her mother's assumption (as Amy sees it) that "I'm just her daughter and that's all she needs to know about me" makes the going lonely. She explains: "Most of the time I'm fine. I don't want you to think I feel this the whole time. But it's always there, and it sometimes surges up within me, this great feeling that I'm moving further and further away from everything that I've known, like I jerk awake and realize I'm on some super-fast train and I don't know where I'm going."

The relationship with her mother, which until recently was "easy," now seems punctuated by confusion. Their responses are out of step. They begin with a glance, or a slight sound: It is a nearly wordless exchange of hope and disappointment.

"What?"

"Nothing."

"What!"

"Nothing!"

The changes rupturing the familiar conversational steps are not so much points of contention as areas of bewilderment. "I see her looking at me," Amy explains, "and it's like she's asking, 'Who are you?' But she doesn't really ask me. She's more comfortable telling me what I need than asking me what I want."

In spite of this, Amy remains exquisitely sensitive to her mother's experience. "She's all wrapped up in this stuff at work, and with my brother, who keeps getting into trouble. It must be bad, because of how she is, and I guess my dad's useless—I mean, that's my mom's word because he can't do anything with Joshua either, and it's like everyone's let her down." Her mother becomes the lightning rod through which Amy experiences all family pain and tension, but her mother will not open up to her, and allow Amy "a chance, you know, to talk it all through and explain that I'm on her side."

The other side of listening, and essential to it, is talking. Girls want mothers to listen, but they also want them to talk. Amy continues to tell me how annoying her mother can be: "I tell her stuff and she goes, 'Mmmm' like she's thinking something but she's not going to tell you what!" Does "Mmm" mean that her mother is only pretending to listen, and is really thinking about something else? Does it mean that she is disapproving, doesn't like what she hears, and is searching for some way to tell her that? "She tells me not to grunt. She says it's rude. It's just as rude to make that stupid noise and not say what you mean."

Amy is quick to criticize what her mother says, but she wants her mother to keep speaking. "She doesn't really tell me stuff. She asks me how my day was and I go 'fine' and I ask how hers was and she says 'fine' and then she blames me for being grumpy, but it's such a stupid conversation. What's the point of talking if she never tells me anything about her stuff?"

Linda, Amy's mother, says, "She jumps on me whenever I say anything, but keeps on at me until I scream. Nothing I say is right. I might as well keep my mouth shut."

But of course mothers seldom do keep their mouths shut. There is too much at stake. Most mothers, like Linda, fall into the trap of opening up and therefore attracting criticism. Linda explains, "Amy wants my opinion, and I say,

'Why are you asking me? You won't take my advice,' and she says she wants to know what I think, and every time I'm stupid enough to tell her, she thinks about what I've said for maybe one minute, and then shrugs and just throws it away. And that's on a good day. Other times, it's: 'I can't believe you said that, Mom. That is the most stupid thing in the world.' So I say, 'Fine, next time I'll keep my mouth shut,' and maybe she says, 'Next time I won't bother asking you' (because this is one girl who always has to have the last word), but she'll ask again, and keep on at me, and then it's the same thing all over again."

So mothers continue to talk, to "open their mouths," and teens continue to criticize and correct them. Girls push their mothers into dialogue. They are ingenious at finding ways to force things to her attention. They rarely give up, and they have little shame about nagging or coaxing until a mother gives in.

So Amy continues to tease and cajole her mother into conversation. She claims to have given up on the "stupid conversations" she has with her mother, but her behavior says otherwise. "What does 'fine' mean, Mom?" she demands. "Did the meeting you were so stressed about go okay?" "Did you wear your new shoes?" "Were they comfy?" "Did people in the office notice?" "Can I try them on?" "How can you walk in these?"

## Knowing Your Daughter

A step toward meeting a teenage daughter's demand for recognition is to see how we may not be meeting it already.

Without always being aware of it, we constantly interpret others. While we think we are seeing what they are "really" doing, we give meaning to their words and actions and gestures that may be very different from those they intend, either consciously or unconsciously. We fail to hear new things because we are reading only the familiar script.

Getting to know a daughter, and keeping our knowledge up to date, is hard work. We see her grow, enjoy proof of her sense of direction and values, and think, "She doing fine. The rough patch is over." Then, the following week, she dyes her hair, pierces her eyebrow, adopts a new set of friends, and declares a consuming interest in punk rock that has obliterated her goal to be an engineer. Or, we may think she knows how to organize her life, has proven her maturity and independence, only to find, three months down the line, that these skills seem to have deserted her.

Of course, we also have pleasant surprises. A girl who seemed so awkward and diffident is suddenly surrounded by lovely friends, with whom she studies and plans community projects.

Most of us do not notice small changes in a familiar person's personality. We sometimes use stereotypes to interpret and explain even those people we love. Family members get stuck with labels that are accurate only at some point and in some contexts. Sometimes these labels stick because they get matched up with an opposite label given to a brother or cousin: hardworking versus bone idle but brilliant; reliable and sensible versus crazy and sensitive; adventurous versus cautious. These are handy labels, which sometimes provide excuses for behavior that we would otherwise find irritating; and sometimes help us to make sense of things by allowing us to put what we see into a familiar slot. But these labels also prevent us from tracking what's really going on with another person and, in particular, prevent us from noticing that someone is changing. The generalizations we make about others deeply affect what we see.

We have preconceptions of our daughter, and sometimes dismiss new doubts she expresses. Perhaps she voices negative views about herself, her future, and her current circumstances, which seem to us unfounded. We think she's great, has much to be grateful for, and has a good future. "Don't be silly," we say, when she says she is "ugly" or "stupid." Perhaps her thoughts frighten us, and we don't want to hear them. In our mind, she is fine, and this image is fixed. Many girls feel indignant when a mother does not know how she feels.

Sometimes we label behavior as "lip," "back talk," "bad attitude," "disrespect." Even when these labels are accurate, they block out other meanings. Speaking out, expressing anger, and complaining are all genuine attempts at communication. Labeling can be a relational violation if we use it to punish someone for saying what she feels.

It sounds shocking to say that mothers stereotype their daughters—but people do stereotype others. It's a survival mechanism, a defense against information overload. Mentally, we can only handle so much information at a time. To absorb new information, we need to place it in familiar contexts. So, while we take in some changes, we often keep mental hold of the broadly familiar pattern. To do this, we interpret what information we get as consistent with what we already know. In so doing, we may discard some information we receive that does not fit our current assumptions. We may impute motives or moods to someone, to keep that familiar pattern in place.

Sometimes we are too distracted to listen and see who our daughter is becoming. Often a daughter's adolescence corresponds with a very busy time in her mother's life. A mother of teenage children is frequently at a stage when her physical and mental energies are at their peak. Her career may be opening out, just ahead. She may be focused on younger children, who are clear and persistent in their need of her, whereas her teenage daughter expresses needs obliquely, and seems to be pushing her away. She may anticipate more time to herself, now that her daughter is older and more independent. Perhaps she has heard that teenagers are trying to separate from their parents, and that the best thing she can do to aid her daughter's development is to "let go," and hence does not see that her daughter is pleading with her to find better ways of understanding and knowing. We need to take stock, and accept that this difficult, feisty, or apparently independent teen still requires our energy and our time.

## Fear of Knowing

Mothers are sometimes ambivalent about getting to know a daughter. Sometimes they feel that if they knew something, they would worry, or they would have to interfere, and there would then be more fights. "Sasha can be so wild," Megan explains. "Most of the time I enjoy her energy, but sometimes it scares me, and I think, What if things are really bad? What if she goes on shoplifting sprees when she's out with her friends? What if she goes around with guys who are too much for her to handle? I could give you a list of 'what ifs' I don't even want to say because I can't bear to admit that I think about them. I'm better off not knowing, because I couldn't do anything anyway."

In Sasha's opinion, this is cowardly, and she drops heavy

hints that she is a girl who behaves badly, just to punish her mother. "I like to make Mom worry. She thinks the worst possible things about me. But she won't ask. Not straight out. So I let her think the worst. If she's afraid to talk about things, then I'll let her be really afraid of what I get up to."

While Sasha tries to rattle her mother, Amy feels ambivalent about her mother's assumption that "I'm just going through what she went through." When Amy talks to her mother, Linda "pulls it all into the context of what she knows about herself, and tells me I'm just like her. It's not that—well, I like my mom, of course, but I don't like being just like her. I wish I could make her see that."

Linda wants to get to know Amy; but, in Amy's view, Linda gives out signals, "that what I'm saying is irrelevant and not really going in." Another indication that "Mom says she wants to talk but doesn't really" is that Linda does not disclose in any detail her own thoughts. The blanket words Linda uses to describe her day shut Amy out. "Fine," as Amy notes, means nothing, because it provides no information. Giving specific information about one's day—what happened, who said what, the highs and lows of the day, the mess-ups and the triumphs—sends the message that you are willing to reciprocate, and that intimate revelations are acceptable. It is unrewarding work, getting a mother to acknowledge you, if you are unable to see who your mother is. A mother who talks about herself is seen as a mother who listens. As Annie Rogers says, "If teenage girls look at their mothers and they don't find a person of strength and integrity with some weaknesses and imperfections who can be real with them—then whom else can they turn to?"[6]

Amy needs the tension with her mother to define herself. Even highly individual girls look at their mothers and see possible futures for themselves. Sometimes this is comforting, sometimes this is inspirational; but girls also want to be different. In part, their desire to be different is specific: I don't want to be so stressed—I want to have more fun; I don't want to be so high-powered; I want to achieve more in my career/be more powerful or confident either within or outside the home. Any girl can give you lists of which characteristics she would like to avoid or emulate. But the desire to be different is also general: There is a common urge to be individual, to be one's self. Uniqueness is part of who we think we are. But it is with a constant reference to a mother that a girl becomes aware of who she is, herself.

When a daughter refutes what a mother says, or criticizes her for what she does, she gropes for self-boundaries. Her argument is: I am critical of you (and you are complacent about yourself) and therefore I have a different perspective and therefore I am different.

If a mother punishes or threatens a daughter who asserts her sense of difference, then a daughter is likely to heighten her opposition. Or, fearing her mother's rejection, she may decide to buckle under, to be "good" rather than authentic. To help a daughter define herself, mothers need to manage unsettling criticism and conflict. Linda says, "I'd like her to open up to me more. And I'd also like to give her more space. But you can't get it right. Maybe things will get better and maybe she'll feel closer to me when she's older. I'm pretty close to my mom now. But this friction with Amy is hard to take."

## Healthy Conflict

Each mother/daughter quarrel is unique. Its impact and meaning are highly personal. The words spoken and the feelings experienced are never the same twice; yet each quarrel carries common themes, including an implicit desire for understanding, and this commonality forms the foundation of a solution. Unfortunately, what often happens is that both mother and daughter feel worse when they quarrel, but neither knows how to change the patterns that have developed. Each responds in the old way, thinking the familiar responses will get her what she wants—yet each knows these strategies are useless.

Sometimes arguments achieve their aims. But, sometimes, they destroy what they set out to achieve. Instead of negotiating a better balance in the relationship, they threaten to destroy it. What parents need far more than the ability to avoid quarrels are the skills to make good use of quarrels.

The skills are difficult to come by. When a teen argues with us, we hear rejection and insult, and, being human, we lash back. We, too, have pride. "How can you say that to me (who has done so much for you)?" and "How can you talk to me like that (I deserve more respect)?" we demand. We may denigrate or ridicule a child in order to remind her of the true pecking order in the family. We may try to put a daughter in her place, or try to frighten her about the consequences of what she is, or isn't, doing. We may be furious at the fear we have to endure when a girl herself appears oblivious to the risks she takes.

In response, the teen lashes back, using a similar strategy: "If you try to criticize/ridicule/ denigrate me, I can give just as good as I get." Or, "If you try to frighten me, I can frighten you more." And if the parent tries to control the teen with a tighter rein, then the teen can always win: "You can give me a hard time, but I can make your life hell!"

All too often, when we think we are arguing about one thing, we are really arguing about something else. When mother and daughter quarrel about curfews or cleaning up, they are often quarreling about love. "Are you able to think about my needs?" one asks of the other. "Are you able to see who I am?" "Why are you attacking me when I am only trying to protect you?" and "Why can't you trust me to take care of myself?"

As each tries to defend herself, each accuses the other of not understanding. Or, one tries to make things better, and restore goodwill, but in ways that just make it worse.

Sometimes profound misunderstandings of the aims of conflict instigate a downward spiral in the relationship.

A mother who ignores her daughter's rough/angry/dangerous side ("I'm not going to pay attention to such nonsense") may find that her daughter shows these aspects more and more. The mother works harder to ignore it; the daughter works harder to reveal it.

A daughter who wants to show her mother that she is capable of taking care of herself does more and more outrageous things to prove her independence; her mother then becomes more restrictive, and more frightened.

A mother gets more and more punitive as her daughter gives her "lip," so the daughter gives her more and more "lip" or "mouth" because she is humiliated by her mother's response. An ever-worsening spiral occurs as mother and daughter each exhibits more and more extreme forms of the behavior that triggers in the other behavior that the other dislikes and tries to control or correct, with behavior that leads to its increase. In the end, each unwittingly encourages in the other the behavior that each is trying to correct.

The harder each works to remedy the situation, the worse each makes it.[7] It often does not occur to either mother or daughter that she should change tactics.

## A Destructive Circuit

Most books about parents and teenagers address problems of keeping one's patience, maintaining one's authority, and enforcing parental discipline. "Understanding teens" is more likely to be a matter of explaining confused (even "crazy") hormone-ridden hooligans who have usurped our sweet children. This book is written on the assumption, first, that neither parent nor teen is crazy, and, second, that parent and teen love each other.

The normal difficult teen becomes the impossible teen through a process of unsuccessful arguments and negotiations. The normal restless teen becomes dangerously impulsive in response to repeated frustration. The normal argumentative teen becomes sound and fury only through repeated failures at being heard. Teenagers do not start out as aliens; they become aliens through a process of alienation. In argument, anger can become entrenched; positions can polarize; empathy can freeze over. It is crucial to remember that, in argument, it is also possible for anger to be defused, for people to reach agreement, for understanding to be achieved.

The basic moves in mother/teen arguments are determined by the context of these quarrels and by their aims. Though this feels like a hostile environment, it is a loving relationship.

## Learning to Fight Well

Girls need to learn how to fight. This is far more important than avoiding fights. They can learn that it is safe to have their say, that it is okay to show anger, and that they can change others' views through their own words. It isn't a calm and sunny relationship with a mother that gives a teenage girl the strength she needs. A good relationship is honest and open. When people we care about deeply are honest and open, we are sometimes shocked and sometimes hurt by what we hear. But through what we hear, we learn who they really are. Pain and consolation are essential moves in the mother/daughter dance.

But fighting with daughters has rules.

The first rule is to avoid humiliating a girl.

Shaming a girl by outlining her faults and listing previous mistakes will reinforce divisions between you. Girls list "being judged" as among their pet peeves with parents. Judging and listening are mutually exclusive.

Teens are sensitive to anything that belittles them or minimizes their views.

This includes common words of comfort, such as "You'll forget all about this in no time" or "You're too young to be serious about this." The teen hears: "Your experience has no validity" or "Your sense of what you are feeling is mistaken."

By listening, mothers validate a daughter's experience. Listening is a way of saying, "Yes, this makes sense to me" (which is different from "I feel the same" or "I know just what you mean").

Validating goes beyond responding objectively to something, or responding to just what's been said.[8] For a mother to validate the daughter, she takes what her daughter is saying in the context of what it means to the daughter, and what hopes or fears a daughter is expressing through what she says. Girls may enact false persona, or feign far more confidence than they feel. They want a mother to respond on two (not always consistent) levels: to who they are now, and to who they think they will become. They want a mother to pull out all the stops in getting to know them, and they want a mother's unquestioning admiration both of who her daughter is and who she will become. When a teen argues, she is seeking confirmation of a parent's interest in both her high-blown fantasies and mundane concerns.

It is often useful to skip over the point of contention and focus on something positive. An offer to help with practical things, such as getting her the school supplies she needs, washing her sweater, giving a lift to her or to her friends, getting her a magazine or book you know she would like, can shift the argument deftly to one side, and confirm a parent's involvement in her day-to-day interests.

Teens want to understand our position and to discuss it; but they don't like giving way, and losing face.

Persuasion is more effective if a different perspective, rather than a counterargument, is presented. "What about looking at it another way?" is more likely to be accepted than "That's ridiculous!" or "That's not how it is."

When you strongly object to something a daughter says or wants to do, explain your response in terms of your feelings and beliefs ("When you talk to me like that, I feel you are turning away from me" and "When you do that, I worry that you're too angry to listen to me") rather than "You have a bad attitude" or "That shows you have no judgment."

Other examples could be:

"When you lie, I get scared: I'm hurt that you feel you can't tell me, and I'm terrified when I feel I can't trust you."

"When you don't come home at the time we agreed, I worry that something's wrong. That's why I get so angry."

The next step is to deal with the feelings quarrels inevitably give rise to.

The close identification between mother and daughter means the mother can quickly pick up on and mirror a daughter's negative feelings. So a daughter's anger ignites anger in a mother. This increases the heat of arguments, and leads to the mother feeling emotionally flooded by the daughter's hostility.

Some mothers resent the fact that their daughters can let their anger rip through the house, while they, as responsible adults, feel compelled to control themselves. They, too, experience daily frustrations; but, for the sake of others, they contain their feelings. Why should a daughter be able to unsettle everyone as she throws her frustrations around so freely? Megan explains, "Sasha can be all over the place, screaming and stomping like fury, and then she calms down, and everything's supposed to be fine. Everyone else is supposed to forget her tantrum, just because she has. If I lose my temper, I worry about what I've done to other people. I worry I'm setting a bad example. I worry that I'm a bad person. And basically, I feel ashamed of myself if I really lose it. When Sasha keeps egging me on, I think, 'Why should she be able to be so mad and not me?' and I end up shouting at her for being selfish and inconsiderate."

Perhaps, if Megan were to state her position as clearly to Sasha as she does to me, then her quick-witted daughter would widen her eyes with appreciation.

Another problem in keeping our cool is that we don't always know when we are angry. "I do try to stay calm," Linda says. "When Amy starts on at me I take deep breaths, and I think I'm under control—but then I open my mouth to speak and suddenly I'm shouting."

When someone we love is vehemently criticizing us or rejecting what we think we are offering her, we feel crushed, cornered, humiliated. It is virtually impossible to think straight and to be fair to someone else when your heart is racing and your adrenaline pumping. Physiologically, you are overwhelmed. In overarousal, you defend yourself, but you can harm the relationship. It doesn't matter that what you are most afraid of has a basically altruistic/loving source. You are afraid of your daughter rejecting you and of losing the valued relationship.

We have to acknowledge our own anger when we argue, and we have to learn to track it. Sometimes we feel gloriously self-justified when we are flooded with mind-blowing adrenaline. It can be helpful to take one's pulse in the heat of the moment, and then at two-minute intervals, to see how long it takes for our pulse to slow—which is a crude but fair indication of whether our body has calmed down.[9] If we believe we have calmed down but still have a fast heart rate, we are highly susceptible to taking on any heated emotion a daughter expresses. So, if a daughter is still angry when we resume our talk, we pick up the anger as well, defeating the purpose of the time-out.

## A Positive Reminder

The mother's past care, and the daughter's child-love for the mother, may stand as a shadow behind her, but it also lights the way toward her future. Her fury toward the mother's habitual views is double-edged: "I am no longer that needy child you think I am!" she wants to shout, but she also wants to say, "Show me who I can be! See me as I want to be! Without your acknowledgment of who I hope I am or will be, I won't believe in myself."

Even as the teenage girl insists that she wants to answer all important questions herself—in particular those about who she is and who she wants to be—she seeks her mother's acknowledgment. "See me as I am!" and "See me as I want to be!" are her persistent and often unspoken demands. She wants a mother's recognition of who she is and a mother's faith in who she will become. When a mother responds to her bid for a new identity, the "argument" spurs her confidence and growth.

# 3.  *"Let me live my own life!":* *Why Teenage Girls Are* *Insulted by Parental Concern*

**ENOLA** and her daughter Vera, sixteen, sit side by side in the front of the car. Vera, a learner driver, is behind the wheel. Enola's eyes are on the road, elbows at her side; she is intent on assessing her daughter's driving but avoids giving unnecessary instructions. Vera seems the more relaxed of the two. Her attention moves easily from the street to her mother. Their argument is not yet full-blown, but something started to simmer the moment Vera informed her mother, causally, that she had to eat supper early because she was heading for a friend's house, where she and her friend "can catch up on things."

"What things?" Enola asks.

"Soaps and stuff. Josie videoed them."

"You want to go to Josie's?"

"Yes, I want to go to Josie's."

"I don't know about that."

"I want to go to Josie's after supper. What on earth is the big deal?"

"Last time you went to Josie's you weren't back until midnight." Enola's voice is deliberately steady. The reminder aims at neutrality.

"It wasn't midnight! It was maybe eleven-thirty. You just don't like Josie."

"There are a lot of things I don't like about Josie."

"Here it comes!" she says under her breath.

"I don't like how you behave when you're around her or after you've spent a lot of time with her."

"Why?" After a pause, she demands, "Just how do I behave that you don't like?"

"Veer—I don't want to talk about it now."

"You don't want to talk about it, or you don't have a good reason why I shouldn't go."

"It's a school night. It's already five o'clock. I just don't want you to go."

"And I just want you to stop messing up all my plans and interfering with everything I want to do."

Mother and daughter are now ready to enter battle. What are the terms of engagement?

## Terms of the Argument

It is tempting to see the distinctive feature of adolescent and parent battles as a struggle for independence. A teen wants to "live her own life," and a parent prevents her from doing so. In adolescence, young people develop complex reasoning skills that allow them to criticize and "see through" many of the adult arguments that once countered theirs. Now they are wise to many of the ways of the world, and often respond skeptically to parents' so-called wisdom. In the course of a few short years, they have developed a range of skills that allow them to plan and act independently. So, why are parents still checking up on them and giving them orders about what they should be doing, with whom, and at what time?

Ask any teen, and you'll be told that the problem lies with her parent.

"My mother is the most annoying person in the world," fifteen-year-old Anna declares. "She's ruining my social life. I can't go anywhere without her knowing everything. If I'm a minute late she goes berserk: 'I thought you were dead/ how could you do this to me?/ you know the rules/ all you had to do was call.' She thinks I'm totally incapable of taking care of myself. But I'm more streetwise than she is. I know how to walk through a rough neighborhood in the dead of night and keep trouble at bay. If she only had one ounce of faith in me, we wouldn't have so many fights."

"To hear my mom talk, you'd think I was the dimmest thing on earth," Charmaine, fourteen, explains. "She thinks I'm going to go into a club and disappear, like I'll merge with a bunch of rave-crazed maniacs. She thinks every party is some black hole of drugs and death. She thinks anyone who has a pierced tummy is going to die of AIDS. She thinks I've never heard of a condom. According to her, I'm some delicate little reed with no backbone. If she trusted me, we would get along just fine."

Vera, Anna, and Charmaine are confident of their competence and judgment. When they reflect on a mother's "interference" and complain that she tries to control them, they put forward their own trustworthiness as the overriding issue. They blame a mother's failure to appreciate their good judgment as the source of the problem. The solution, in their eyes, is simple: Their mothers should have faith in their judgment, and then there would be no conflict.

This assumption covers their own self-doubt as to how capable they are of self-protection.

## Why Offers of Help Ignite Anger

When a two-year-old expresses outrage at being helped with some task, such as buttoning a shirt or tying her shoelaces or opening a door, she is protesting against the interference of her mission to learn how to do something. She is focusing on her aim, and hates to admit that she is failing.

A teenager's frustration at "help" or "interference" is similar, but also significantly different. When a parent offers help, it is not because a daughter lacks the necessary fine motor skills or physical coordination. It is not because she is not tall or strong enough. It is because her parent is simply in the habit of helping her.

"Stop telling me what to do! Can't you let me do it myself!" Vera shouts when her mother offers to take her to the airport to visit her father.

"I was only offering to help. You don't have to shout!" Enola yells back. Yet offering advice or help unsettles Vera because she is in part fighting her own internal response, which whispers, "Can you really manage by yourself?" So when Enola asks Vera whether she is sure she is okay going by herself, Vera explodes. Enola's anxiety enlarges the remnant of self-doubt Vera herself is trying to brush aside, as she plans to take the trip from Chicago to Cleveland to visit her father. She wants to stamp out her own doubt, and her mother's protectiveness ignites it.

After all, self-doubt is easier to deal with if we blame someone else for it. We take what is internally troubling and create it outside ourselves. The problem is still there, but it's the mother's fault for treating her like a baby. If it's the mother's fault, then the teen does not have to feel inadequate herself for feeling, still, like a little girl, in need of her mother's watchful care, or powerfully moved by a mother's sympathy, anger, or concern.

But although teens present the issues as simple and clearcut, their strategies reveal their own awareness that they are standing on shaky ground. They exaggerate and distort a parent's position in ways that would stretch a hole in any argument. Anna describes her mother, Lisette, as "going berserk" when she is "only one minute late." Anna imputes to her mother the belief that she is "totally incapable" of taking care of herself. Charmaine says her mother thinks she is "the dimmest thing on earth." The mothers' actual positions, which are far more measured and moderate, are ignored as the daughters argue in order to create a screen around their own self-doubt.

But face-to-face with a mother, girls use different tactics. They key into what a mother is actually saying, find her weakness, and attack it. As Enola carefully weighs up her wish not to start a fight against her reluctance to let Vera go to Josie's, Vera senses that her mother does not want a fullblown argument. As soon as Vera gets wind of this, she moves boldly forward, showing that she is ready to do battle. Not being afraid of a quarrel, she is more confident and more aggressive. With a teenager's faith in the power of voice, she argues that her mother's reluctance to articulate her reasons for not wanting her to go is a sign that her mother does not have a good reason for her objections.

## Why Teens Love to Argue about Rules

Packed within conflicts is proof of a mother's hard work in setting rules. It is agreed between them that it is not enough for anyone to say "You can't do this because I say so."

Instead, there has to be something like "a good reason." "I'm telling you you can't do this because it's dangerous/inconsiderate/disruptive/unwise/impossible to organize" frame parental rules based on reasons rather than mere authority.

This style of rule setting has been shown to encourage more self-control in children than do either authoritarian styles of rule setting ("Do this because I say so") or permissive parenting ("Do whatever you want/think best").[1] If a parent is set up as the final authority, without a framework of reasons to support and explain parental rules, then a child is less likely to develop a framework within which she herself sets rules outside parental control. Permissive parenting, which sets up the child as an authority, presents judgment as intuitive or idiosyncratic, rather than conclusions from reasoned arguments. These two styles, authoritarian and permissive, have been correlated with teens who are less good at self-control.

But the reason-based style of setting rules, which is correlated with greater self-control, nonetheless makes life much harder for parents. Children then learn that rules have to be justified. So, as soon as they become competent arguers, they demand that parents give reasons for their prohibitions. Enola's good parenting skills lead to more work as a mother of a teenager who continues to demand "Why? Can you justify what you say? Here's my justification. What's wrong with that? My argument is better."

Vera's acute knowledge of her mother, and her belief that one should speak one's mind, add to her mother's workload. She demands to hear her mother's full thoughts and to engage with them. She casts the challenge "Tell me what you're thinking, and let me judge whether your reasons are justified. I have something to say about this, too."

Teenagers are so good at criticizing others' arguments that their own, to them, have a luminous certainty. But the skills a teen has to think for herself are more idealized than real. Often she is better at picking holes in arguments than putting together arguments of her own. And, often, one reason behind the prohibition is: "You're not capable of dealing with what might go wrong here." Then it comes down to "Yes I am!" and "No you're not!"

## Why Don't You Trust Me?

Within a girl's complaints about her mother is a continuing need for appreciation. She complains about a mother's interference because it shows that she does not have faith in her judgment. The issue at stake is not simply whether Vera can go out after supper. The issue is what her mother thinks of her. While Vera claims she does not care what her mother thinks, she demands, with the air of someone insulted, "Why don't you trust me?"

Once a mother takes this on board, she can make sense of why the temperature rises so quickly. However, recognizing that your daughter is hurt because you do not trust her judgment, or do not share her global confidence in her ability to "look after herself," does not solve this problem. Understanding a daughter's perspective is not enough. There is real substance to a mother's fear that a daughter cannot look after herself.

Parents frequently describe their teenager as irresponsible, reckless, and lacking common sense. Sometimes mothers see this as a sign of rebellion. "If she gets an idea into her head, there's no way she'll let go of it. My saying 'no' is like a red flag to a bull. She wants it more than ever," Enola explained. She, like many mothers, also fears the influence of Vera's friends. In Enola's eyes, her daughter's judgment has fallen prey to her friends, "and anything I say is just so 'uncool,' it just doesn't figure."

Enola is worried about what has long been called "peer pressure." Fearing ridicule from friends more than she fears the consequences of joining them as they snort cocaine or accept a lift from a stoned driver, a teenager goes with the flow. Vera acknowledges that she sometimes does feel pressure to do what her friends are doing, "even if it's something I might not, by myself." Nevertheless, she presents this as a rational choice. "I hate being left out. My friends are all doing stuff. We share things, and I don't want to miss out. I can always say 'no' to this and that. I often do. And my friends have respect. If I say I don't want to do stuff, they're cool with that. Things aren't nearly as bad as my mom thinks. And I can handle all the things I do."

Perhaps Vera will not know how pathetic this argument is until she hears it from her own teenage daughter. In the meantime, her mother has to fight to persuade her that she is under more pressure than she acknowledges, that she faces the same risks as anyone else, that she cannot handle any more than anyone else.

Some parents fear that a daughter's poor judgment is a sign of her low self-esteem. Lisette says, "Anna can be so impulsive. It's like she has no inner control, and doesn't care what happens to her, doesn't really care about herself. And she won't hear me out! There's some nervous white noise rumbling in her head that drowns me out." Lisette notes that a teenager who does not care about herself, who, in other words, lacks self-esteem, does not care what happens to her, and therefore does not take care.

Anna complains that her mother doesn't see who she really is; but the real problem is that Lisette sees more than Anna. Lisette says, "She thinks I can't see beyond my own nose. Look at her. She's tiny; she's a coil of nervous energy. She flits from one passion to the next. Sometimes it's a boy. Sometimes it's a girlfriend. Sometimes it's a rock group or some band or other. But I see it as all the same thing, one replacing the other. She needs something to steady her. There's a kind of desperation that I'd give anything to help resolve, but she won't open up to me. Like I'm supposed to be taken in by that superficial cheerfulness. I tell you, that girl is desperately unhappy, and I don't know why and I don't know what to do about it. She races around to find some distraction, and really she doesn't seem to care if she hurts herself as long as she doesn't have to face whatever it is that's bothering her. So what am I supposed to do? Am I supposed to sit back and say, 'Well, if my daughter wants to wander the streets at any time of night, that's her business?' Am I supposed to stand back and let her get hurt, just because *she* doesn't care?"

Taking care, being careful, caring for oneself have very different meanings to a parent and to a teen. Parents know that even if they can't give the exact statistics, the number of car accidents involving teenagers is high. They know that the incidence of pregnancy and sexually transmitted diseases is higher than it should be, even among teens who are well-informed about birth control and safe sex. They know how a girl's confidence can be bashed by girlfriends who taunt and tease, or by boyfriends, who flirt and then flee. The mothers in my study were aware of a range of dangers to their teenage daughters, and were bemused by a teen's inability to perceive the dangers.

Ada, Charmaine's mother, says, "Char is a great kid. I'm really proud of her. She'll take anything and anyone on. I wish I'd been like that at her age. I know she'll go far. But she has to get through this first. She has to stay alive, for one thing. She has to graduate. She has to avoid being messed up by drugs. And then wouldn't it be nice if she went to college? Wouldn't it be a real plus if she didn't get pregnant? But can I tell her any of this? I try, but all I get is how much she knows and how little I know. I might as well be singing in the wind. She knows it all. Or that's what she thinks! Somehow, she knows that her friends are never going to crash a car. Somehow she knows that she can do whatever drugs she does and stay in control and only take this poison when she wants to. How many other girls have thought that? Hmmm? How many? Well, Charmaine doesn't care because she has it in her mind that she's the one who's different from everyone else. Bad things don't happen to her. Well, isn't she just the lucky one?"

Mothers, in despair at a daughter's apparent inability to act in her own best interests, describe a girl as "thoughtless" or even "stupid." They accuse her of having "tunnel vision" or of "just not being able to think one sensible thought." They also accuse her of "not caring what she does to others" and "not caring about what she does to herself."

A daughter so accused feels outraged: She does care, she is responsive to and does feel responsible for others, she is highly sophisticated in her account of the effects of her actions on others.

Charmaine says, "Mom should know better. She knows I think of other people and my future. The whole time! That doesn't mean I can't live now! She has these warped ideas about what I should do, and she doesn't bother listening to me."

Her mother says, "I can't not care. I can't see her falling into this slump and worrying about nonsense things and wasting time with kids who make her feel inferior without saying something. But her view of a good mother is someone who lets her teenage daughter do whatever she wants and never worries. She sees some perfect mother who wouldn't even dare to wonder what her daughter's up to."

And Charmaine replies, "As you get older you start to do things by yourself and I kind of see my life that way, and suddenly I get stopped by this person who thinks I have to do what she says. The idea that I don't know myself what I should and shouldn't do is just my mother's excuse to interfere."

## Smart Teens Can Have Poor Judgment

Charmaine, Vera, and Anna are proud of their newly acquired life skills. Yet there is one crucial area in which girls their age have not yet developed, an area in which they may in fact be less well equipped to find their way than they were as ten-year-olds who trusted others to guide them. In her newfound intellectual confidence, a teenage girl lacks the ability to assess her own weaknesses. The area in which she flounders most is that of assessing risk. It is this weakness, and her blindness to it, that terrifies and terrorizes a parent.

Adolescents can argue well. They are capable of complex and abstract thinking. They are good at applying general principles to particular cases. They have splendid imaginations. But they are inept at assessing risk, especially when they themselves are involved. Youth feels immortal. With its energy, its certainty, and its love for its own promise, it seems indestructible. A teen often doesn't see the risk she is taking because her imagination is not yet equipped to conceive of her own death. Her sense of self is so acute that she cannot conceive it being obliterated.

We all, at any time of life, have trouble taking on board the fact that inevitably we will die, but as we mature, we live with this fact. At least we know we can die, even if the reality of that fact evades us in our day-to-day thoughts and plans.

The acute self-consciousness characteristic of adolescents, who constantly worry about their "looks" and whether or not they fit in, provides them with an imaginary audience. Teens find it impossible to do anything without feeling they are being looked at. Each minute of her waking day, someone is watching, assessing, judging, commenting. This imaginary observer both plagues and protects her. She endures constant anxiety as to whether she looks "cool" or dumb. The threat of embarrassment is as unsettling as the threat of war. But it also blinds her to the notion that one day she will not be seen, or that she will one day not be a self-observer. Death is a fiction, which she can only imagine with herself in the audience, and in the audience, she is still alive.[2]

When someone does not believe death is a real possibility for her, then what seems dangerous to most people will not phase her. But the central cause of adolescent risk taking, is a teen's cognitive failure in dealing with the laws of probability. She simply cannot assess risk.

Recent research using new techniques to monitor the growth in teenagers has found that certain areas in the brain—cortex areas that are specialized for "executive functions" such as planning and self-control—do not mature until

one's early twenties.[3] The brains of teens are, in some physiological ways, immature. Your daughter may have a very
grown-up physique, but, as new scanning techniques have
revealed, those parietal and frontal lobes are not yet mature.
The gray matter in these parts of the teenage brain grows
dense, and only later scales back to mold a leaner thinking
machine.[4] These are the areas of the brain that deal with
self-control and planning. So, your teen has a short fuse; she
forgets to clean the yard or to keep that appointment with
the optician; she has a totally different take on risk and danger than her parents because, while her body seems mature,
while she is capable of rational argument on some abstract
points, she is not mentally equipped to organize and regu-
late herself.

Revelations in brain development may provide new evidence, but they do not provide new information about what
teens can and cannot do. Parents have known this all along.
Teens are not good at assessing risk.[5]

Vera is not alone in thinking she can "handle" what no
one can really handle. What seems a clear danger in the eyes
of an adult may seem safe or safe enough to a teen. If a girl
has done something a few times without ill effect (driven too
fast, driven after drinking, taken ecstasy, had unprotected
sex), then she believes it is safe. If she sees a friend do similar things without ill effect, then she also believes she has
evidence to squash the killjoy arguments of the grown-ups.
In addition, she exaggerates how many times she herself has
gotten away with something or how many of her friends are
engaging in this behavior without suffering any harm. "All
my friends take Ecstasy" may mean that a few people she
knows take it regularly. She may insist she knows what she

is doing, when she is acting on uninformed impressions. It is not surprising therefore to hear a mother say, as Ada does, "I can talk until I'm blue in the face, but I won't get her to pay any attention. Short of locking her up, I don't know what I can do."

This standoff results from opposing views—of mother versus daughter, adult versus adolescent—views that cannot be incorporated into a single frame. Teenagers are indeed what others would call reckless; but in their view, they reflect, consider, and assess. While some parents think that a teen doesn't care whether she hurts others, or doesn't care whether she hurts herself, the problem is often that she does care, but cannot assess the likely consequences of what she does.

There is, then, no difficulty in explaining why mothers "interfere" with their daughters' lives. They interfere in order to guide and protect. They fear the dangers on the street and on the road that could, in a flash, inflict irreparable physical harm. They fear the malign influences in lifestyle that could destroy mental and physical health. They fear others' carelessness toward the girl they see as the most precious thing on earth. Maternal protectiveness is hard-wired into us and needs no complicated explanation. It is what teenage girls make of this input, advice, and control that creates confusion. In a teen's view, maternal protectiveness is at the very least a nuisance, and it is often a crime.

### How Daughters View their Mothers' Fear

"My mother is afraid for me to have fun."

Teenage girls tend to resent a mother's fear. "The best thing about growing up," Anna tells me, "is that I'll be able do things without asking anyone's permission. I won't have to deal with her absurd fear about what might happen to me the minute I'm out of her sight."

A mother's fear seems a mean plot against the lives these girls want to live. Over the course of the past twenty years, many women, reflecting on their growth to independence, have described how hemmed in they felt by a mother's sense of danger. They report hearing, and having hated, the messages: Sex is dangerous; the streets are dangerous; men are dangerous; friends can be dangerous; rapists lurk in the corners of a dark street; drugs will be foisted on a young girl who goes to a rock concert. A mother constructs the outside world as dangerous, it is argued, either because she does not want her daughter to go out (and wants her to stay home, to stay close, to remain her mommy's child); or, there may be some more malign reluctance to see her daughter have fun, or develop as an individual; perhaps envy of her youth leads to resentment at her having any fun at all.[6]

A daughter sees the fear as unnecessary, yet she feels infected by it, and therefore she resents it. Any mention of fear is like an old record, and it hampers her lifestyle; it's an unnecessary drain on her energy and fun. The teen's version of a mother's control is the Rapunzel story: The wish to lock her in a tower once she hits adolescence is the wish of a jealous witch, not the wish to keep safe something so precious.

## The Mother's View

"Short of locking her up, I don't know what I can do to keep her safe," Ada says in despair.

A daughter's sense that she is "fine" and "knows how to take care of herself" is often countered by a mother's belief, based on a teen's poor assessment of risk, that she is setting out to hurt herself. "How can you do this to yourself" the mother cries, her impulse to protect outraged by a daughter's recklessness. The daughter dismisses this concern with "I know what I'm doing" or, even less convincingly, "Leave me alone."

The teenager's job is to experiment. Adolescence is like a permission slip society gives to young people: You may be physically mature, but given that it takes so long to prepare for human adulthood, we give you an extra space few other creatures have. During this time you can test your beliefs and your skills; you can learn about yourself and reflect on how you want to fit in to this complex society. Teens develop a sense of their capabilities by means of intellectual and physical adventure.[7]

Unfortunately, healthy exploration and foolhardiness are not always easily distinguished. And a parent's aim is to protect as well as to foster growth. The balance is always difficult. When does our protection constrain growth? If we restrain her, do we limit her imagination? When we warn her of danger, do we burden her with unnecessary fears?

The difficulty of gauging this balance is that we do see dangers where teens do not. We also hold their physical safety to be of paramount importance; whereas to a teen itching to explore herself and her world it is discovery rather than safety that is her priority. Girls, too, may experience greater controls than boys. Both mothers and fathers tend to be aware of a variety of dangers in a teenage girl's sexuality—the mother, from her own experiences, the father, from memories of his own responses to teenage girls, and for both, the fear is informed by awareness that girls' sexuality speaks its own language, and may invite responses from others that could harm the girl.

Mothers today often have a sophisticated sensitivity about the risks a daughter faces. They are aware that young girls may be pressured by others, that even a feisty daughter who is happy to take on a mother and father, and resist their wishes, may comply with the wishes of others. She may, too, be ill equipped to define her own wishes and inclinations as distinct from those of a peer, whose approval she seeks and whose abandonment or ridicule she fears. A mother may be aware that her teenage daughter may be under this pressure from others, and that this will put her at risk. A mother will also know that her daughter will not admit this to her, and may not even realize herself that she is dependent or compliant. Aware, too, of the dangers of low self-esteem, and how this may push aside self-care, mothers often see a girl's risk-taking behavior as an expression of anger, despondency, or a general failure to care about herself.

The mother's experience of this conflict can be read as a version of Little Red Riding Hood: The carefree girl in the forest cannot gauge the evils that beset her; she overestimates her own ability to judge others and is, therefore, easy prey for wolves.

## Maternal Tactics

There is a gulf between the ease with which a parent can control a child through reasonable fear and the frustration a parent experiences as she tries to convince a teen that what she is doing, or plans to do, is unsafe. Teenagers are not the only people in this relationship who fight dirty to get what they want.

Sometimes parents are so terrified for a daughter, and so

helpless in the face of her determination to defy them, that they use anything at all to regain control. They distort facts and statistics to terrify the daughter.

Steph, sixteen, has been planning to go to a New Year's Eve party with four friends. This is the first New Year's Eve she has had the freedom of having friends who drive. Earlier that day there was a snowfall, which is now freezing hard. Her mother, Delia, looks out of the window and decides that Steph cannot drive with her friends. "It's too icy. The roads are just too icy. I'm sorry. I know you've been planning this. But it's just not safe for an inexperienced driver."

So far, this is a good textbook approach. Delia is firm, explains why she is taking this line, expresses regret for her daughter's disappointment, but stands her ground. For Steph, this is not good enough. Steph panics at the notion of being left out of this shared experience, of letting her friends down, of being the odd one out, the one who can't join in. She is also enraged at the abruptness of the change: First she could go, now she can't. Her first tack is to challenge the details of her mother's argument:

"Doug is not inexperienced. He's been driving for nearly a year. He's a good driver. He is not inexperienced."

"Steph—"

"You don't even know him, and you're judging him!"

"Your friends can come here."

"My friends don't want to come to this stupid house where there's nothing to do with all these crappy people hanging around."

"I can go out now and get whatever you need. Whatever . . ."

"I don't need you to do anything! I can't believe this. I'm going out with my friends."

"Not if it means that a sixteen-year-old boy is driving."

"He's seventeen! He's been driving for a year!"

"Steph, I wouldn't want to drive in this weather. I wouldn't trust anyone who was willing to drive in this weather."

Steph begins to weep with rage, mourning over the lost evening. She is frustrated at being, still, a kid in her mother's house. Delia tries to comfort her, to negotiate something further, but Steph stamps her foot, leaves the room, and then slams her bedroom door. Half an hour later, she comes out, ready to go. She picks up her keys, gets her coat, and does not respond to her mother's questions. Delia then says coldly, "Okay, go. Go ahead. Drive out with your friends. The road is ice. You'll have a great time when the car slides off the road and you and your friends are scarred for life. That will be a night to remember."

Many mothers describe being at their "wits' end" in trying to get daughters to confront the dangers they are facing. Their distortions are symptomatic of their sense of impotence. They exaggerate because more rational arguments seem to have no effect.

If we could reflect, at a safe distance from our own fear, we would understand that a daughter keys into the distortions, hears them, and resents them, even as she does her best to feign indifference.

"When my mother goes on like that," Steph explains, "telling me how sorry I'm going to be for doing what I want to do, I just go rigid inside. It's like a nightmare—you know you're standing in a tunnel and there's a piercing sound of a train that keeps coming at you. That's how her voice is—this sort of siren that's drilling through my head. She gets hysterical. How can I take her seriously? I don't even feel like answering back. There's no point in telling her I'll be careful, or we won't go out if the roads are really bad. She's not going to listen to me when she's in that state. I feel like making monkey faces at her—" and she tucked her tongue inside her lower lip to puff it out and began scratching herself, monkey fashion—yet she was too angry and heated up to laugh at her own antics.

Steph responds to her mother's panic, not to her arguments. She sees her mother's desire to control her, not her urge to protect her. She catches her mother out in her irrational certainty that she will be in a car accident. There might not be an accident: Therefore, her mother is wrong; therefore, she is right.

Like each mother/teen argument, the one that occurs between Steph and Delia on New Year's Eve is a variation of a common theme: How far can a girl be trusted to protect herself, and when does a mother have to step in? This is a question Delia has to confront in many contexts.

Ever since Steph was diagnosed with juvenile diabetes at the age of six, Delia has tried to allow her "to lead a normal life. That's what I always wanted. And I told her not to be afraid, that there was nothing to be afraid of as long as she ate right and did the monitoring thing and the injections. I didn't want it to be in the forefront of her mind. But now she's not afraid enough, you know? I don't want her to be afraid, but I want her to have some sense. And she has no sense.

"Years and years, now, I've been asking her about those glucose levels and the shots, and we've been going to checkups together. Now she says she can do it all herself and I should butt out—but I don't know. Maybe I've played things so she doesn't realize how really dangerous it might be. Things I've never before said to her about what could happen, things I could barely say to myself, I now want to shout at that girl: DON'T YOU KNOW WHAT COULD HAPPEN TO YOU? She had more sense when she was six than she does now that she's sixteen."

Indeed, children do seem to have a better measure of risk than teenagers. While children are not brilliant assessors of probability and risk, they have a concrete sense of danger. "If you *touch* a knife, you'll cut yourself." "A car will smash you to bits if you cross the road there." Of course, young children are impulsive, and do act without thinking. Parents have to work hard to teach them that they should be afraid, even while they have to tell them that if they follow certain rules, life is safe enough. When a child takes this on board, when the rules and regulations necessary to safe-enough behavior are taken on board, then a child is allowed to cross a street herself and to find her own way around the kitchen. But teens need to do a range of new things for themselves, by themselves, and perhaps, in consequence, minimize the risks.

"My mother thinks I should follow her advice, like I'm better off making her mistakes than mine," Steph explains to me. "I can take care of myself. She uses this condition as an excuse to baby me."

## Finding a Balance Between Fear and Trust

Many mothers describe the difficult balance between fear on the one hand and respect of a daughter's privacy on the other. They fear that something is wrong, and that the daughter does not want to speak about it; or they fear that something is hidden, and they need to discover this in order to help and protect.

Charmaine's mother was taken by complete surprise when she discovered her daughter was cutting and burning herself. It was Charmaine's younger sister who saw the cuts on her sister's stomach and told her mother. "She didn't want to tell me," Ada reports. "She tried not to, and she kept it to herself for over a week. She was crying when she told me because she felt so bad about 'telling on' her sister, but she was too worried not to. And I guess I did the worst thing possible. I marched into Char's room and said, 'I want to see your stomach. You lift up your shirt," and she of course was furious. I could see that flare of hatred that I sure remember feeling when I was her age. You know, that homicidal urge you have when your mother makes a scene? But there are some things you can't let go. The last thing I want is to damage what's between us, but I was in such a state."

Charmaine herself said, "I'm—oh, I'm too mad to speak. I could spit. I feel so—violated. No, I can't talk now. I don't want to talk to anyone. And never, never will I tell my stupid awful mother anything."

Here hot issues of trust come in: "You are prying because you want to interfere with my life; you can't do anything to help me, so why should you have to know everything?" Whether it's self-harm or drugs or sex or shoplifting or cutting classes, girls respond to a parent's need to know as a mean bid for control rather than as a maternal mandate to help. The anger at a parent's "snooping" drives a girl to a rage of self-righteousness, or, as Ada notes, inspires "that homicidal urge," even if she is "guilty" of the parent's worst fears. Her heartfelt defense is: "It's wrong to have someone looking through my things/reading my diary/accessing my e-mails/forcing me to speak." If they are hiding something, they feel they are handling it; once a parent swoops down and uncovers it, teens lose control.

Mothers feel awful when they "snoop" or "spy," but they do so because they are frightened about what they don't know.

Charmaine is ashamed that a private act of resistance (a very ineffectual one) is exposed to her mother's eyes. Her self-inflicted injuries strike her as brave at the time she does them, but under her mother's gaze, they are pathetic. Her mother's hysteria makes her ashamed.

"It's bringing one world crashing down on another," Charmaine says. "I'm a different person on my own and with my friends. I can't be that person with my mother, and then she comes storming in saying, 'Ha! I'm going to catch you as you really are and destroy you.'"

As I wait for this description to sink in, Charmaine modifies it. "I guess she just wants to help. But she can't help, and when she gets on my case I just feel smothered."

There are two very different stories. There is a daughter who sees that her mother has committed the crime of invading her privacy; the presumption that the mother has a right to know everything is something anyone with a mother wants to counter: "You don't have a right to know! I have a right to my privacy."

But anyone who is a mother knows the other story, that of Ada's panic: "My heart was beating. My mouth was dry. I couldn't swallow. I couldn't think. I was saying to myself, 'This isn't happening,' but I was also saying, 'This is the truth and it all makes sense and I have to have it out in the open.' And then the fight was not about self-harm but about her privacy. Char was right, but she was also totally off base."

This is an eternal dilemma. The tension between the need to protect on the one hand and a daughter's call for privacy on the other cannot be easily resolved.

## How to Interfere When We Have to Protect

So what can we do when we need to "interfere" because we need to protect a daughter—from herself, from her friends, from her environment?

An initial exercise is to discover the extent of the offense one has already committed by "prying" or "interfering." What makes a daughter most angry about such infringements of her privacy is a parent's self-righteousness. The message "I know I have a right, and don't tell me otherwise" creates a breach between mother and daughter. A girl is more likely to relent if she hears "This was a tough call, and I don't think there is a clear right of way, but given how I feel and how much I care, I decided to do this, and I'm very sorry that it has offended you, and I can see why it has offended you."

Once a bridge has been built, a further exercise is to ask a daughter for her views first. "I know you are angry with me, and I see why. But I'd like to understand more. Could you tell me how you feel?"

She will want to have her say; she will want to complain about her mother's behavior. It is important to hear her out, take in her perspective without defending yourself with counteraccusations.

Then, we can explain the basis of maternal panic. A mother has the best chance of staying close if she shares her fears and ambivalence with her daughter. These fears are best expressed directly, as "This is what I'm afraid of" rather than "This is what could happen" or "This will happen."

Then, a mother can acknowledge to her daughter that everything involves some risk, and that she accepts this. What she is interested in discovering is whether her daughter can name the risks of a particular activity.

One sign of listening and being willing to understand is asking the right questions. The right questions can also trigger awareness in the person who answers them. If mother and daughter continue to disagree on what risks are acceptable, a mother can go further and explore, with her daughter, why the girl finds risks acceptable:

Does she take risks because she does not see them as risky?

"I find what you are doing too great a risk. Do you agree that there is any risk in what you do?"

Or, does she take risks because she does not think that she is subject to the usual risks?

"Do you see the risk, but think it won't happen to you?"

"Do you see the risks, but take care to minimize them? How?"

"Do you think the risk is worth taking? Why?"

A daughter can show us what she does understand, thereby proving the point about her trustworthiness; she can also learn to see the shape of her mother's fear, and a mother can exhibit her willingness to listen and appreciate her daughter's capability.

If she persists in behavior that the mother sees as reckless, then work with her to identify the reasons:

What to her are the risks of not engaging in this behavior?

Does she fear that she will miss out on a shared experience?

Does she fear that others will exclude her?

Does she fear that others will ridicule her?

Does she fear that she will be letting others down/disappointing someone?

Does she fear she will miss out on developing skills/doing something she values?

Ideally, neither mother nor daughter should view this discussion as a battle. Escaping the argument mode is difficult when maternal protection and teenage excitement are in conflict. Teens are keen arguers. They are spin doctors, working at presentation, ignoring fine points of honesty. Keeping to the points at issue, and controlling our own fears, are constant challenges in parent/teen debates.

# 4.    *"She can pick an argument out of thin air!"* *What Lies Behind Teenage Irritability*

**WHEN I ASK** mothers and daughters what they argue about, they are quick to list the familiar causes of conflict: They argue about rules (what, whether, and when they can go out), they argue about grades and studying, about friends, and about responsibility (in managing time, money, personal safety). But when I observe their quarrels, I find that many seem to arise out of nothing and, while heated, prolonged, and recurrent, seem to be about nothing. A mother and a daughter are chatting easily, then, suddenly, the clouds darken, lightning strikes, and thunder is not far behind. A mother asks a question, bites into an apple, utters an exclamation of concern or pleasure, and her daughter cries in rage, slams the table, storms out of the room. Far from being in the midst of a battle about rules, responsibility, or values, mother and daughter whip one another with complaints about tone of voice, turn of phrase, and familiar gestures.

"All I have to do is take one step too close to her, and she growls like a lion," Pam reports of her thirteen-year-old daughter, Margot. "She complains that I am 'in her space' if

I stand behind her to see what she's doing on the computer. She wriggles her shoulders, even if I don't touch her, like 'ooh, get your cooties away from me.' She can't stand to hear me breathe. She once burst into tears because the way I was drinking my coffee was annoying her so much that she just couldn't bear it."

Margot admits that "there are times I really want to scream just, maybe, because, you know, there's that little clicking sound at the back of her throat when she swallows, and I know it's mean, because she has a right to swallow, doesn't she? Usually I leave the room when I get upset like that, and she doesn't see it, because I don't want to blow up over that, and I can't say I understand it, except I know it isn't just me. My friends get annoyed by their mothers too, I mean really annoyed, so annoyed that you can't think straight."

This is a common theme in girls' complaints about a mother: Mothers are annoying. What annoys a daughter can be so minor that it is hard for anyone to find a link between the innocent action and the furious response. Alex says, "The minute she comes in the room, I tense up. She stands there like, 'You can ignore me. I won't disturb you.' But I can't concentrate with her there. It drives me nuts."

"She's impossible!" declares Vicky, Alex's mom. "Always barking at me, wishing she could keep me up a tree."

"Mom, that's not true!" Alex is both amused and hurt by this description.

"You have some other mother? Hmmm?"

"No."

"Then I'm right. Because that's how you treat this one."

Alex is fuming at allowing herself to be led into a position that gives her mother the last word. Vicky is angry because she is hurt. The argument is about love and rejection. In a private interview, Vicky underlines this:

"Every little thing I do sets her off. I used to like going into her room. I could sit while she played or read. She would turn her head around, maybe smile at me, and just go on with what she was doing. I liked hearing her hum to herself, or she'd make these little exclamations when she played on the computer. It was so restful. I could hear her rustling and breathing. Sometimes I'd have a five-minute nap. She paid me no mind. Now she freezes up. She says I distract her. She can't think. She can't concentrate. I walk into a room, and I can feel her squirm."

There is a special way that people who are close to you can annoy you. In Vicky's view, you have to dislike someone an awful lot to find her basic physical presence offensive. "It rattles me. And I catch myself through the corner of her eye: I'm this woman who commits a crime just by being alive."

## When Knowing Someone Too Well Can Be a Comfort or a Curse

When we know a person very well, her presence is sufficient to call up a host of feelings. Whether in love or in hatred, one view is all we need to call up a range of responses. This is why the company of someone we love is so pleasurable and can provide instant comfort, and why the presence of someone we dislike or loathe can be so immediately grating, darkening our mood in a flash. Embraces and fights can begin before words are spoken; and what seems to be the cause of either a sparkling conversation or a draining battle may be a pretext for either. Someone walks in the room, and our feelings rise up, ready-made. Unable to explain this, a girl blames her mother for something she said or did.

A mother's physical presence exerts a powerful force on her daughter. The touch and sounds of a mother's body have a long history. In infancy, a mother's body provided the basic needs of life itself. In early childhood, it was essential to her sense of safety and wholeness. Now, in adolescence, the feelings are mixed. The teen feels trapped both by the comfort she is inclined to experience in a mother's presence and by her wish to expel the previous child-self who once welcomed the comfort. The power of that presence remains, but its meaning changes. Now it draws her back to all that she wants to leave behind. She wants to feel safe and whole without her mother. She wants to feel grown-up. The echoes of comfort and dependence her mother's presence continues to provide can be confusing, out of keeping with her fragile, wishful sense of self. And this is the starting point in the argument that seems to be framed by the challenge "How dare you still be alive!"

## Mothers' Uneasy Memories of Their Own Teenage Irritability

There is nothing quite like the ferocity of a teenage girl's irritation with her mother. Vicky says of her daughter Alex, "It's as though there is some awful monster inside her. Every little thing irritates her. She growls and scratches her way through breakfast. You can feel the hostility when she walks past."

Vicky finds her daughter's anger unpredictable and unfair: "I never know what is going to set her off. I never

know when she's going to scream about something I say."
Vicky is alarmed because she sees Alex's irritability as "bad
attitude," and all the things that could go with that. "Dissing"
her mother means not taking her advice, not following her
rules, being out of control.

The difficulty of having her daughter appear to hate her
is compounded by memories of how she hated her own
mother. "It's no good to say 'I was mean to my mother, and
now I can see I was wrong,'" Vicky says. "I still feel angry
with her about some things. I still think she was impossible
about some things. But at the same time, I can see how
unfair I was to her. I can't believe I'm as awful as my mother
was. But when Alex tells me I am, I'm not so sure." Her lin-
gering judgment against her own mother haunts her as she
confronts her teenage daughter's ferocious irritability.

But it is Alex's abiding love that leads to this irritation.
Ambivalence about how close she feels to her mother
becomes a complaint about her mother, and a quick trigger
for a quarrel. Sometimes this uneasy ambivalence links up
with other more easily recognizable issues of conflict. Alex
explains that when she asks her mother whether she can go
out, or whether it's okay to come home at a certain (late)
time, she can feel her mother's reluctance "inside me." If her
mother says, "Oh, all right," she still feels "that my mom
doesn't like it, and that messes up the whole thing and I feel
bad and then I get even angrier with her because she's making me feel bad inside when all I want to do is have a night
out with my friends. I feel bad about it, but I still want to
go, and if I stay home, I'll hate it, so I go—because, why
shouldn't I?—but I get this ick feeling."

Alex feels uneasy at her abiding need to feel she's okay
with her mother. Her love draws her close, but the closeness

interferes with her independence. She seeks a space that she herself cannot find. Her confusion is expressed as rejection, which makes her mother afraid she is losing her daughter's love. The quarrel then is not only about going out or staying home, but also about the quality of love.

## The Power of a Look

Teenage girls, as we have seen, complain about not being understood, or heard, or seen. They also complain about being seen or watched. Here, three girls ascribe daily violations they think a mother commits by seeing them:

"Just the way she looks at me is enough to drive me around the bend." (Ashley, fourteen)

"She stares at me, and it's as though she's getting inside me." (Margot, thirteen)

"Her eyes are like peelers stripping me away." (Alex, fifteen)

If a person's physical presence can have a strong impact, think of the power her glance can have. Exchanges between mother and daughter are splattered with challenges: "What are you looking at?" "Why are you looking at me that way?" or just "What!" as an outraged exclamation in response to a mother who has focused her gaze on a daughter.

To a child, a mother's face represents a mirror. The recognition and delight, the concern, fear, or disapproval displayed in a mother's face provides a reflection: This is the meaning of what I am and what I've done. There is no such thing as a look without meaning—especially from mother to daughter, who have compiled a dictionary of glances. A child looks to the mother to see who she is.

In adolescence, she finds new mirrors. These include

friends and other teen idols. A passionate awareness of her independent future sets her priorities. Her highly individual judgment is in the process of rapid growth. While many girls are content for this exquisite individuality to be influenced by friends and consciously chosen role models, they guard it from a mother with the ferocity of a lion guarding a cub. But a mother's view, and the array of judgments and questions that can be packed into her glance, continues to wield its profound power.

For the teenage daughter, a mother's mirroring is no longer straightforward. The plague of self-consciousness makes teenage girls relive, over and over, a difficult situation. Their memories are highly visual, and they are at the center of what they imaginatively "see." The worst aspect of being self-centered in the way teenagers usually are is the expectation that "everyone is looking at me critically."

This is experienced as raw exposure, very close to the description given by the psychologist Erik Erikson of the experience of "shame." He writes, "Shame supposes that one is completely exposed and conscious of being looked at: in a word, self-conscious. One is visible and not ready to be visible; which is why we dream of shame as a situation in which we are stared at in a condition of incomplete dress, in night attire, 'with one's pants down.'"[1] While shame signals self-dissatisfaction, it is often expressed as rage at those who are looking. Feeling unsure, the teen rages against the person looking at her. And to whose "look" is she most sensitive? The mother's, of course.

A harsh critic of her own looks, unsure of her ability to fit in or look cool, she is also a harsh critic of her mother's behavior and appearance. A mother breathes too loudly. She has a host of annoying habits, such as scratching her cheek when she gets nervous, or pressing her lips together when she is uncomfortable with what's being said. In public it is worse, because everyone else will be catching out her mother's flaws, too, and condemn the teen by association. Mother/daughter identity makes a mother hateful because she can so easily embarrass her daughter, at a phase during which embarrassment is seen as the worst possible of human conditions. Anything that makes her mother distinctive is a flaw; anything noticeable about her mother should be hidden.

This exquisite adolescent self-consciousness changes her relationship with everyone. She is no longer so self-absorbed that a mother can sit in a room with her while she draws, writes, reads, or plays on a computer. The mother's mirroring becomes a distracting illumination. Everything she does is writ large. "What are you looking at?" is a cry of accusation. "Why are you looking at me?" means "Why are you judging me?" It does not matter that at this stage a girl is very likely to discount her mother's judgment. Her mother's eye is still a powerful force. She feels both known by the familiar person, and not known, because she herself is changing, and knows her mother sees that, but what meaning, she asks, does it have to her mother?

## *"I can't be myself when you look at me."*

It is now commonplace knowledge that observation changes what's observed—and that is certainly a girl's experience when she is aware of being observed by her mother. Some girls say they feel inhibited in a mother's presence. They can't be who they are. The self in relation to the mother is so powerful that they lose their sense of that different self they are beginning to develop with friends or teachers or employ-ers or passersby. "She never pays any attention to me" is something mothers often say of a daughter; and while in one sense it may be true, in many other ways, it could not be less true. A daughter cannot ignore her mother's presence.

At eighteen, Lan is an aspiring actress who describes the nuances of her response to her mother's gaze.

> I can't concentrate, not when I'm onstage when she's in the audience. Not the way I'd like to, or the way I usually can. I can rehearse at home, with her around. She helps me learn my lines, I mean she really helps me. She just keeps feeding me them until I can spout them off by heart. But if she's in the audience, in a real performance, it's distracting, like something's tickling me. I imagine what she's think-ing—that she's thinking I'm great, that I'm marvelous, and I'll hate her for being so excited. Or, I'll imagine that she's criticizing me, thinking I didn't get the phrasing or empha-sis right. All these things she does with me are helpful until the play actually begins. Then I don't want her anywhere near me. Not at least until I'm really famous and have my own fans! I guess that sounds pretty mean, but I think I can make her understand.

A mother's gaze is an unwanted mental magnet, pulling a teen's attention, impeding her freedom. In other contexts, she may find her mother's attention helpful. Informally, in practice, she works with her mother. The particular mater-nal intimacy of her help is clear from Lan's language: her mother "feeds" her the lines, and makes sure they get inside her. Lan then "can spout them by heart." The input is useful and empowering.

However, there is a limit to the value of this input. In a

"real performance" Lan wants to put her mother to one side. Until she is sure of her professional identity, she does not want to be distracted by her mother's gaze. While she understands that this could be interpreted as ungrateful, or as a rejection, she believes she "can make her mother understand."

Lan, in late adolescence, is at a transition point. Instead of blaming her mother for simply being alive and looking at her, she identifies how her mother sometimes helps and sometimes hinders her. Instead of getting angry, she tries to make her mother understand. While younger teens often feel passive in response to a mother's looks, older girls often express confidence in managing their ambivalence. This confidence usually comes with practice, much of which involves the hit-and-miss of quarrels.

## You Make Me Feel Like a Baby!

A mother's familiar mannerism, or phrase, or facial expression can set a teen's anger alight. Perhaps once she thought it was normal, part of the maternal bedrock. Now she feels split between the familiar and accepted, on the one hand, and the sense of being new and individual on the other. The familiar turn of phrase or exclamation pulls her back to a child response, which she wants to escape. The customary smiles and greetings now seem patronizing.

A toddler may feel anxious about leaving her mother. Will she be all right if she runs from the bench to the sandbox, all that distance from her mother? Will she be safe? Will her mother be anxious? As she walks toward the other children, she looks back at her mother. She is smiling. She is delighted by her independence, and this makes the toddler feel confident and blessed. In the teen years the impact of her smile can turn a mother into a criminal.

"How dare you smile at me as though I were still a kid!" is one common response from a teenager.

"I hate the sickly pleasure I start to get when you smile at me" is what they mean.

"You're treating me like a baby" may actually mean "I feel like a baby in your presence."

The habitual gestures of sympathy and reassurance also spark irritation. Margot's mother, Pam, says, "The worst thing is I can't comfort her anymore. I can't get near enough to put my arm around her. Like today, she came home from school and went into this big mopey story about how diffi-cult everything was, and—oh, I don't know, something about being friends with someone who was cutting another girl she liked, and she being caught in the middle—and she went on about that, and you can just feel her unhappiness twist-ing her around, and I went to say, 'Aw, come on now,' and she turned on me and shouted that I was treating her like a baby, and she might have been breathing fire she was so mad."

Margot is like a patch of dry timber eagerly awaiting any word from her mother to burst into flames. "I wish she'd just leave me alone. She never leaves me alone. I feel she's try-ing to get inside me."

A mother's sympathy can wake the needy, pathetic child that the adolescent is trying to suppress. A mother's hug or sympathy or fear or concern can make that younger self rise up and choke the tough, confident teen. So the teen, furious at the strength of this inner child, shouts at the mother: "You're babying me! You can't see I've grown up! You think I'm still your little girl! You don't know who I am!"

She feels overtaken by the child-self, and blames her mother. The mother sees her fury and thinks, "What did I say?" and then says to a friend, "I just open my mouth, and she snarls at me."

In mother/daughter interactions, the meanings invoked are often rooted in a girl's past responses. A mother asks a checking-up question, and the daughter feels like a little girl again. "Do you have your keys?" or "Do you have bus money?" may seem like neutral questions to a mother, but to a daughter the implication is "You're not able to look after yourself." These questions could be easily tolerated if uttered by a caring friend, but from a mother they pinch on a girl's own doubts. She knows she sometimes forgets things. She knows these small lapses in forward planning can lead to enormous inconvenience—when she has to walk home, or get a lift from someone she'd rather not be in a car with, or when she has to wake her mother to open the door. Feeling threatened by the girl who can't remember to pack her lunch, take her keys, or put money aside for the bus ride home, she blames her mother for reminding her of her child-self.

"I can't make her see what she's doing to me, Ashley says. "Little things, or things she thinks are little, will make me so angry. She asks me stupid things, like which bus I'm getting, or—she does this whenever I take my bike out—do I have my lights? And then sometimes—it's so stupid—she asks whether I think my hair clip is going to stay in! Yeah, she asked that this morning. Really! 'Is that hair clip going to be okay? You don't want to lose it.' And she just looks at me, as if to say, 'What's up? What's your problem?' She makes a suggestion or something, maybe just about what I should wear, and she puts me in such an awful mood. She doesn't see how bad those little things are. They can ruin my entire day."

As Ashley speaks, she makes fists with her hands, which she beats rhythmically against her thighs. She is angry with her mother for having such a strong effect on her and not understanding why. She is angry with her mother for suggesting that the problem lies in Ashley's touchiness—a suggestion that heightens her irritation, because Ashley cannot say why she is angry. Her mother unwittingly evokes an old self that Ashley is trying to discard.

Alongside these subterranean responses based on a personal history too complex, at any one moment or in any single situation, to articulate is an urge to test out herself as an agent—basically as someone who can do things herself. This is the irritable two-year-old writ large, someone who may not do things just as her mother would have her do them, but who wants to do them herself.

"If I stay in her sight line for more than ninety seconds, then I know she's going to give me some of her stupid advice," Ashley complains.

A daughter delves into each maternal response like a dressing-up drawer and uncovers a wealth of imagined responses. Then she criticises each in turn. Any word or sound has meaning that then breaks the thread of thought and imposes an element of uncertainty on the task at hand. A mother's shrug can drain the pride from an achievement. A mother's doubt or hesitation can threaten to topple her confidence. The shadow of fear on a mother's face can darken her anticipation of an outing. A teenage girl, keen to follow her own wishes and act according to her own judgment, can be defeated by a click at the back of her mother's throat.

## *"Just the sound of her voice gets on my nerves"*

Some girls describe an invasion of a mother's voice; they carry around, as part of their mental furniture, her habitual sayings and stories and warnings. Unable to rid their minds of her images, they blame her and stand in opposition to her, while the real battle is within themselves. A mother's voice seems louder and stronger than their own. That is, very often, why they shout. It makes perfect sense to the daughter, but is nonsense to the mother.

Many girls carry on imaginary conversations with their mothers. They hone their own script. How should they tell her this? they wonder. What might she say in response, and how will they answer her?

Pam says, "I can walk into a room, and Margot will shout at me like we're in the middle of a fight. And I just got there! So I say, 'What's going on? Why are you yelling?' and she just does her heavy breathing act."

Margot says, "I can hear her voice when I do stuff, like she's there even when she's not. It's not like I think she's really talking, but I think what she'd say. Maybe about what I'm eating, or when I buy something, I imagine how she'd criticize me—you know, 'Why do you eat that junk when you think you're too fat?' And sometimes it's nonsense stuff about tiny things that don't make any sense. Sometimes I imagine myself going at her and pushing her down, and hitting her."

Imaginative teens describe their mother's voice as a constant commentator. They run their own private version of what a mother is "likely" or "bound" to say. Or, they may be thinking that they are actually keying into a mother's thoughts, but they are overinterpreting the meaning of her words and gestures. A hesitation, a change in the rhythm of her breathing, a tensing of her shoulders, a nervous twitch of her foot—these are all spotted by the keen and critical eye of a daughter. Arguments arise as she second-guesses what her mother is about to say, or what she is thinking. "Why don't you want me to go?" or "You never want me to have fun" or "You don't understand" can be a daughter's response before her mother has said anything at all.

In fact, this is one of the most important reasons for allowing a quarrel to occur: The daughter confronts the real mother's voice, which is likely to be very different, and more responsive, than the broken record inside the teenager's head.

## "How can I avoid irritating her?"

There is no way to avoid a daughter's irritation with our natural rhythms of speech and movement. We cannot reprogram ourselves. "Being careful" with a daughter, "watching out," "holding our tongue" seldom avoid trouble. However quick a girl is to lash out at her mother for a spontaneous word or gesture, she is more ruthless in dealing with studied, practiced moves in the mother/daughter dance.

Girls are exquisitely sensitive to a mother's tone of voice. They can spot a "prepared speech," thereby rendering useless the care a mother takes in thinking through what to say. Our well-prepared efforts get sliced into little pieces as a daughter mocks us simply for trying.

Pam has been thinking about what to say to her daughter Margot about the time she has been spending with her friends versus the time she has been spending on schoolwork. She wants to be tactful and firm, but without "laying down the law"—something she knows her daughter hates. She has decided to frame the discussion by soliciting her daughter's own assessment of her values and future hopes, and plans to follow on with a discussion of what Margot should do to honor those values and reach those goals. Pam will remind Margot that she herself knows she has to balance schoolwork with her social life.

What could go wrong?

Pam chooses her moment carefully. They have finished eating supper. Neither mother nor daughter is hungry or tired or rushed. They fit neatly into the routine of washing the dishes and putting things away. The music played by Pam's younger son can be heard in the background, a reassuringly normal sound rather than a disturbance.

"I want to help you think about your priorities," Pam begins. There is a steely silence. She continues, "Do you still want to go to college? I mean, is that still a goal? Because if it is, I think—well, I think perhaps you should think about the way you're spending your time."

"Yes, Mom."

"I really think—"

"Yes, Mom. I can tell you've been really thinking about this, really hard, and have worked out how this is going to pan out, and ten minutes from now I'm going to see the error of my ways and never go out and never worry you again."

Knowing a parent so well, a daughter can spot the subtle changes in her voice when she speaks from a text. As Margot explains, "My mom takes in a deep breath and speaks in this staged voice and starts parroting stuff, you know stuff that must come out of some cretinous parenting book, and I just want to shout: 'Who do you think you're kidding!' She's trying to be in control, but the script is so stupid. It's pathetic!"

And Ashley, while less confrontational in her mother's presence, broods over "things that my mom does that really annoy me" in her absence: "I hate it when she starts to make a speech. She takes in a deep breath, and sort of straightens her back like someone's about to take her picture, and she starts to talk in this voice. She even sneaks sideways looks at herself in the mirror. She thinks she's such a smart mother, and I can just feel her inwardly congratulating herself. It's yuck! It's like I'm this child who has to be managed and she thinks she's doing it so well, but she's crap."

Teenage girls are ruthless observers, and seldom give a mother the benefit of the doubt. They don't want to be duped by a parent's pretense, and they are frustrated by a mother who has one eye on someone else's script. They can tell at once if a mother has rehearsed her words, or if she has a hidden agenda. At the same time, a mother's spontaneous expressions and speeches will also, at times, rouse a daughter to a high pitch of irritability, just because they are so typical of her mother and so familiar.

## How Can We Deal with a Daughter's Irritability?

What can a mother do about having to breathe? What can she do about the power of a glance or word or sigh? How can she address these criticisms?

Teens respond to a mother's presence through a layered history. In one sense, nothing can be done. A mother cannot engage in these battles, because her daughter is not shouting at her so much for what she is doing in the here and now but for all that she has meant to her daughter in the past. How is she to deal with that?

- We can show her that her "rejection" does not damage the relationship.

    A daughter's rejection, in the form of irritability, is a request for some space and time. By not punishing her for her irritation with us, we prevent this momentary response from escalating into a series of quarrels about her "bad attitude." She is, after all, not being totally unreasonable. She is fighting the impact we have on her. She makes this internal battle into a battle with her mother. This makes the conflict easier to tolerate.

- We can talk to her when she seems to be arguing with her own idea of a mother who seems to have little to do with us. We can help her locate the real problem. Setting aside our unsettling responses ("That's how I feel toward someone I really dislike" or "That's how my mom made me feel!") we can focus on a daughter's internal struggles by inviting her to talk about them. We can ask, for example, "What's bugging you? I really do want to know. It may be obvious to you, but it's not to me. I'll wait while you think about it, and you can say anything you like, because I really want to understand."

- We can challenge the voice she carries inside her head, the imagined maternal mutterings and comments that we ourselves may have little to do with. One exercise is to ask her what she thinks you would say during some nightmare mother/daughter scenario: if she came home drunk, was arrested for possession of drugs, shoplifting, reckless driving, if she were suspended from school? Then tell her what you think you would actually say, in the heat of the moment, and what you would like to say, and what you would be feeling.

- Take on board that her apparently unreasonable irritation

is not a sign of bad character, or of hatred, but just part of a teen's complex negotiations with her layered history of connection and dependence. By assuring her that the mother who loved the child is also the mother who wants to understand how to love her changing teenage daughter, we can diminish her fear that in loving us she has to stay a child. However slow we are, in her eyes, at learning who she is, we can persuade her to be our teacher.

# 5.
# *Power Struggle:*
# *The Choreography of Status*

**WHEN MOTHERS** and daughters argue, each feels an utter clarity of purpose, yet we can see over and over again that the aims of each are complex and often hidden. Arguments are about the teen/parent issues we think we know about, and they are also about profound mother/daughter themes: connection, recognition, respect. At the heart of the connection theme is the question: "Do you still love me?" Recognition involves acknowledging change from the child to teen, and differences between mother and daughter. Respect includes validation, authorization, and idealization: I hear what you are saying; you can speak your mind; I believe your thoughts and needs are centered within a wonderful growing person.

But, in the midst of a daughter's need for connection, recognition, and respect on the one hand and a mother's impulse to offer these on the other are two human beings staking out their own turf and guarding their pecking order in it.

"Don't you use that tone of voice with me!" and "I'm not having language like that in my house" are bids and battles for basic respect. A mother's insistence, "You'll do as I say" and a daughter's threat, "If you don't let me do what I want to, I'll make your life hell" feel like terrible power struggles, but frequently signal a vitality in the mother/daughter relationship as each negotiates her status in relation to the other. The status each is either jostling for or protecting is complex and transient. It has little to do with normal status issues between women (who's smarter/more popular/nicer). Instead, it is shaped by the following questions: Who has a right to tell whom what to do? Who needs to be reminded of what? Who is being honest or open, and who is covering up?

Here is one example, among a myriad in any day, of a mother and daughter in a series of minor conflicts during which they negotiate status relative to each other.

Naomi, fifteen, is working to finish a woodworking project that is due the next day. Her mother, Joyce, is preparing dinner. There has been a brief exchange about time management and cooperation. When Naomi's mother came home from work, she was distressed to see wood shavings all over the kitchen table. Sullenly but dutifully, Naomi cleared them away while her mother began to prepare dinner. "Are you going to lend a hand here?" Joyce demands, but Naomi explains she has to finish the project that evening. "And how long have you known about that?" Joyce demands, but Naomi does not reply. "Just get your work done," Joyce directs her daughter—an order that is actually a concession: She accepts her daughter's priorities of finishing the school project rather than preparing dinner. Some time later, Naomi brings the wood box into the kitchen to show her mother. She hands it to her. As Joyce reaches for it, Naomi draws it away with the warning: "Don't touch it. It's not varnished yet. I have to take it apart again to do that." Joyce wipes her hands clean, but does not reach for the box again. She looks at it, and nods approvingly. Naomi puts the box aside, crosses her arms in front of her and announces, "I had an awful day, so don't annoy me."

Joyce: "Aw. What was so bad?"

Naomi: "Everyone's been really yucky and horrid. And Debbie—grr!—um—she's always showing off, like she knows what's wrong with everyone, and she's telling everyone I'm sucking up to the chemistry teacher."

Joyce: "So? What do you care?"

Naomi: "I don't! Except—oh, you don't understand. There's no point—see, I had to stay after class in chemistry to clean up."

Joyce: "What did you have to clean up?"

Naomi: "Just some stuff. I was doing this experiment with Jo, and some ammonium chloride spilled."

Joyce: "You spilled it?"

Naomi: "Yes, Mom, I spilled it. It took like two seconds to clean up, and that's not the point."

Joyce: "Were you in trouble?"

Naomi: "No! I wasn't in trouble." (Her voice exaggerates a goody-goody tone.)

Joyce: "Mmm."

Naomi: "Don't say Mmm! I hate it when you say Mmm."

Joyce: "Oh, Naomi!" She takes a deep breath. "Okay, you weren't in trouble. 'Okay,' not mmm, okay?"

Naomi waits four seconds before picking up her story.

Naomi: "So I come out, and Debbie says this thing about

sucking up and looks at me—and I don't want to talk
about it."

Joyce: "So don't talk about it."

Naomi grimaces at her mother. Her mother's face freezes.
They stand in silence for several seconds, while Joyce continues to run water over the lettuce.

Naomi: "Do you want some help?"

Joyce: "You can peel the carrots."

Naomi stands by the sink beside her mother, nudges her
with her (higher) shoulder, and looks down at her, and says,
"Shrimp."

This is a near-quarrel, apparently about very little, just
edginess about the number of things to get done, and bad
moods at the end of a working day. Following the moves of
mother and daughter, however, we can see big issues at work.
Even without a hot topic of argument, an atmosphere of accusation and criticism prevails. What is also clear is that Naomi
contributes to the repair work, which ends the conflict.

The conversation has a harsh start-up. Naomi warns her
mother that she is in a bad mood. This warning is also an
implicit accusation about her mother's tendency to annoy
her. At the same time, she expresses a need for interest and
sympathy because she had an awful day. Joyce responds to
the appeal for sympathy, and ignores the implicit rebuke.

Joyce invites her to talk about it ("What was so bad?") and
Naomi accepts this. As she talks about friend problems that
have made it an awful day, her mother tries to help her by
offering her avoidance advice: "What do you care?" implying
that she should not care about people's judgment when they
say things that are not true. Naomi hears this advice as useless criticism. This is a sign that her mother fails to

acknowledge how much she does know, and, anyway, she's not going to take advice from her mother. "I don't" is an identity reminder (a reminder to her mother about who she is now) more than an agreement to what's been said.

The information Naomi discloses is, for Joyce, a window onto her daughter's life at school. She seems to be checking up on Naomi's behavior and her status at school, which is not why Naomi tells it. She answers, but also mocks her mother's concern. It puts her in a child's position. She retaliates for being put in that position by shouting at her mother (for saying "Mmm"), a habitual expression of her mother's that Naomi hates. Naomi's mother shouts back. The shout "Oh, Naomi!" becomes a warning not to take this further. Mother and daughter are then at a temporary standoff. But the mother relents (she takes back the "Mmm" and replaces it with something more palatable ("okay").

Having given way, Naomi's mother is not willing to give way again when Naomi cuts off her own narrative with "I don't want to talk about it." Joyce does not extend her invitation to talk. She accepts what she says ("So don't talk about it"), but this acceptance of what her daughter says is really a cold step away from her daughter. Joyce pointedly refuses to respond to Naomi's emotive message, and replies only to the straightforward meaning of her cry, "I don't want to talk about it!" Naomi then mends fences by asking to help prepare dinner. Her mother, in accepting the help, accepts the gesture to repair the relationship.

But Naomi won't let the status quo go unquestioned: She walks close to her mother and measures their respective heights and reminds her mother that she is now the taller (and that her mother is a "shrimp"). Joyce does not challenge this reminder of her lower status, and accepts the physical closeness as a reminder of connection. The tension eases; they are at peace, but Naomi insists on keeping the status she has gained.

## On the Edge of Understanding

For Becky, fifteen, and her mother, Sharon, the renegotiation of status is less smooth.

Becky's conversations with her mother are awkward rituals. Even before each speaks, one answers the other with a look that half forms a question, then, when no answer is forthcoming, each blames the other for not listening or not being willing to talk. It is a poignant, nearly wordless display of hope and disappointment.

Becky: "Um?"
Mom: "What?"
Becky: "Oh . . ."
Mom: "Yes?"
Becky: "Nothing." (mumbles) "Telling you wouldn't do any good."
Mom: "What!"
Becky: "Nothing!"
Mom shrugs; Becky glares.
Mom: "If you have something you want to say, you can say it."
Becky: "If I had something I wanted to say, I would say it. I don't want to talk to you. There's no point."
Mom: "Fine. Then you can unpack the groceries and put them away. And DON'T even think about opening the ice cream."
Becky has picked up a grocery bag, but now slams it down. "I wasn't going to! I wasn't going to!"

Mom: "For heaven's sake. Don't shout at me. Just—just go to
    your room and clean it up. I don't want your help in here.
    I don't need your attitude right now. I have enough prob-
    lems of my own."
Becky: "Fine! I don't want to be here either."
Becky kicks the grocery bag, which is now on the floor, and
storms out of the room.

Sharon initially assumes a mother's role of listener, trying
to persuade Becky to say what's on her mind; but while
Becky goes halfway toward expressing a wish to speak, she
also sends her mother the message "Telling you wouldn't do
any good." Sharon then gives up that position to swoop down
to a lower status, telling her daughter that she has more
problems. She leaves her mother-platform to complain per-
son-to-person, to say, "I have enough problems of my own."
Superimposed on this uneasy argument is an altercation
about who can speak out and who can understand.

This is yet another of the many mother/daughter fights
that isn't about what parent/teen fights are supposed to be
about. It is not about curfews or schoolwork or boyfriends or
drugs or money. It arises in a context of a daughter who feels
misunderstood and a mother who feels rejected. The more
familiar teen issues of eating habits ("and don't even think of
opening the ice cream") and messiness ("just go to your
room and clean it up") arise incidentally, as ballast in the
more basic conflict.

Sharon feels rejected by her daughter. She wants to help,
but to do this, Becky has to open up. Becky is not sure she
can open up. She may feel this isn't the right time, or perhaps she worries that she herself does not have the words for
what she wants to say. Sharon becomes impatient with this

hesitation, but Becky then blames her mother, accusing her of being incapable of understanding. Her message is: "I have something to say and I'd like to talk about it but really, on reflection, there's no point."

From Becky's point of view, she has tried to open a conversation with her mother, but something goes wrong. Perhaps her mother is not quick enough to give her full attention. Perhaps Becky detects an edge in "What?" that was uninviting. The daughter is frustrated; the mother is hurt.

The argument then escalates. Hurt by her daughter's failure to talk, Sharon tries to tell her that it is okay to talk. Becky stubbornly refuses the offer. It's a classic double bind: Someone asks something of another, but gives a message that conveys the opposite. Becky cannot disagree with the principle: She agrees that she would say something if she wanted to say it. The cruel implication is that she doesn't want to say it to her mother.

And then things fall apart. Sharon feels rejected, so she starts issuing orders. Telling someone what to do is a simple way of gaining status. But because this is not really what she wants, because the issue is whether her daughter is able to trust her and talk to her, she does not bother to maintain her position. At first she wants her daughter's help, and then, as Becky is about to comply, she issues a negative directive about the ice cream, which unhinges Becky, who then "loses it" and who is then reprimanded for her attitude. There is then a counterdirective not to help her mother but to clean up her room and get out of her mother's way.

In the clear light of day, Sharon can see what should happen. "I look at her sullen face, and my heart sinks. There's nothing I wouldn't do to help her. There's nothing she can't tell me. Anything—really, I'd put up with hearing anything. How bad can it be? I mean, I go through all the awful things, and I think, nothing is so awful, if only she'd tell me."

But her plea with her daughter to speak what is on her mind is uttered as a command, and nothing silences someone as quickly as a command to reveal oneself. The real weight on Becky's tongue, however, is doubt as to how to formulate her feelings. "Sometimes when she looks at me I can feel her thinking, 'What on earth is wrong with that girl?' And then, if I'm stupid enough to try to talk to her, she gets all antsy and starts to tell me I mustn't say this or that about myself, or that if only I'd follow her really good advice (yeah!) I'd feel better. So we don't get anywhere."

Sharon and Becky are like many mother and daughter pairs, each caring for the other, one wanting to explain herself to the other, one wanting to hear, and yet neither able to do this. They argue about status, whereas what they are seeking is connection.

## Arguing over Status

The teen's battle for self-definition and higher status is contagious. Generally, if we feel that the person we are speaking to is using the conversation to give herself status, then we do one of two things. We search for a way of hiking our own status, either one-upping or matching her, or we accept our role in the conversation as status enhancer ("That's terrific!" "How wonderful!" "You must be proud!"). We may, if we take the latter line, expect that at another time, the conversation will take a reciprocal turn, and boost our ego. If the status-endorsing talk is always one-sided, we tend to disengage, and may not seek out conversations with that person, finding them tedious. Confining one's role to admirer or supporter tends to wear one down.

These common rules of conversation, however, do not apply to parent/child talk. With our children, bolstering their egos is a delight. They are so close to us, so much part of us, that we are happy to do this long term. Their virtues and talents reflect well on us, and so our pride in them makes us feel good. Our admiration and support of their egos comes easily: Parents are primed to think their kids are great, to magnify each skill, to see their own child's development as miraculous, and the development of another child as simply normal. Thinking your kid is wonderful, and telling her so, is part of the parenting package.

This paradise of admiration and endorsement is disturbed during the teen years, as a daughter often tries to sharpen her sense of self in opposition to her mother. Whereas a child's cleverness and knowledge reenforce a parent's own sense of self-worth, the adolescent's often comes across as a know-it-all put-down. She makes competitive moves. Her words, tone of voice, and gestures imply: "I know more than you," and "You don't know as much as you think you know." Instead of the heady days in which we were inclined to ask with rhetorical delight, "Who's a clever girl?" fights arise as a mother declares the daughter is "just too sure of herself." No one likes being put down.

The battle for status can infect the entire household. Women who are normally calm and reasonable can find themselves stubbornly holding to a point or argument or rule because the issue has become: "Who is going to win this argument?" or "Who proves herself to know more?" or "Who has the authority here?" The maternal fear "What might hap-

pen to my daughter if I have no control, no status with her?"
is layered with the human resistance to having one's status
undermined. This is one of the awful ways in which a
teenager can make an unreasonable person of her mother.

The quarrel between Sharon and her daughter Becky spi-
rals downward because it turns into a competition about
who can criticize whom more. Mother and daughter each
has a wounded ego, and that makes repair difficult. "Maybe
I'll lie low for a while," Sharon says, as she speaks about her
desire to mend the rift. But she is also worried about coming
together and fighting again. "Our fights are awful; they're
like the worst PMS you can imagine. There's this feeling of
dread through and through." She also worries that she has
damaged the relationship beyond repair. "I have this image
of my own mother being so awful and saying awful things.
I've never forgiven her for a lot of what went on when I was
a teenager. Why should Becky forgive me?"

Parent and child learn to trust their relationship as they
establish ways of finding each other again after the
inevitable moments of losing touch.[1] With a child, the
rhythms are steady, easily found again. With an adolescent, new rhythms, new ways of being in sync have to be
discovered.

## Why a Mother's Concern Can
## Seem to Lower a Teen's Status

Status issues are buried within many conflicts. A mother's
concern can, from a daughter's viewpoint, be a put-down.
When Enola tells Vera she cannot drive her friends to the
party on Saturday, Vera is annoyed at the inconvenience,
and disappointed not to fulfill the role of driver for her

friends, but the strongest emotion is anger at being put down: "Who are you to tell me what to do?" she wishes she could demand of her mother.

When Vera picks up a peach, and Enola says, as she bites into it, "Be careful with that front tooth," Vera reddens with rage. "I know how to eat a peach!" Her mother's warning implies that Vera does not know how to deal with a crowned front tooth that has caused problems in the past. The daughter resents this presumption of greater knowledge.

Each mother/daughter flare-up, however brief, has a history. Vera remembers breaking the tooth while riding a dodger car ride at a fun park. Her father, already divorced from Enola, was spending his allocated Sunday out with his daughter. The day was near an end, but Vera, then seven, wanted one more ride. She was small for her age, but not too small to be allowed onto the ride. As the car lurched, she fell forward and banged her mouth on the metal retainer bar. Half of her proud new front tooth fell off. Vera remembers the pain and the fear, but above all, she remembers her mother's anger.

Enola was furious at Vera's father for letting her on the ride. She was furious at the designer and manufacturer of the car. She was in despair at the damage inflicted on "her perfect, beautiful child." Vera said, "She gets into a state when I get hurt, even a scrape. She has to scream: "Ooh, my little baby, are you okay?" "Are you sure you're going to live?" "Oh, no, my precious baby girl is going to die!"

The maternal panic, which is a sign of care, is an irritant to a daughter. Vera does not want to be as afraid for herself as her mother is on her behalf. She does not want to see herself as vulnerable. On a number of levels, then, maternal care challenges the daughter's status: It revives that infant-self that depended utterly on the mother; it challenges her own claim to be strong; and it assumes that the greater knowledge (of how to do something, how to manage something, and how to avoid danger) resides with the mother.

## Flare-ups

Status jostling often occurs when a daughter steps into the home, fresh from her peer world in which she is on an equal footing with her friends. It can also flare up as a mother enters a home to find it saturated with a daughter's mess or sound. While some quarrels arise when a mother gets on a daughter's nerves because they are together for too many hours during the course of too many days, about 28 percent of quarrels started up within five minutes of a mother or a daughter walking through the door and into the other's space.

Homecoming is idealized as peaceful, but it is often stressful. Pippa comes home late. Her meeting at work has overrun. The dismissive remark of a senior colleague still stings, and she runs through possible retorts to cut him down. The traffic home was heavy, just as she knew it would be because she had to leave her office forty minutes later than usual. As she opens the door she sees mud in the hallway, and a streak of something sticky, probably spilled soda. Her daughter's music system is thumping through the apartment. The note she wrote with instructions for preparing dinner is still on the kitchen table. She calls her daughter's name. When there is no reply, she screams the name and bangs on her door.

Ange is in her room, talking on the phone. Her face reddens as her mother storms in. She puts up her hand, indicating "just a minute," and explains to her friend, "I got to go," clicks off the phone, and stares at her mother. She listens to the list of her crimes, she sighs, stares at the wall for a minute, and then says, "Jees. All right already. I'll clean up the hallway. I'll get dinner ready. Keep a lid on it, will you?"

For the mother, the question is "Who runs this home, anyway?" This is more than wanting some peace and quiet, it is seeking to regain control of the home. Her daughter has been enjoying the home-alone feeling; this is her home, and she can do what she wants. Her mother reminds her sharply that this is not so. Ange here accepts the move her mother makes to pull rank. But she is keen to have her revenge. "You see how she treats me," she spits out, hoping to draw me to her side. "She is worse than impossible."

Ange shows she is angry as she programs the microwave with a series of punches. Pippa returns to the kitchen, seeming refreshed and forgiving after her shower. Pippa makes normal conversational moves, but Ange ignores her. When the meal is ready, Ange puts her plate on a tray, carries it into her room, and slams the door behind her.

"You are impossible!" Pippa yells after her.

"You are horrible!" Ange replies.

When a girl walks through the door, she may find that her mother asserts her status as the person who regulates the home and the behavior of the family: "Where have you been?" or "Why haven't you done this yet?" From the realm of self-control, she steps into the realm in which she has to answer to her mother. The questions disturb her status as an independent person.

Few parents are aware of just how many requests or instructions or commands they make. When asked how many times a day they tell a teenager what to do, they are likely to estimate that they issue six or seven instructions a day. But trained observers, in home settings, record mothers making on average more than seventeen requests per hour.[2] A teenager who wants to strike a more equal balance with the parent is up against a lifetime's habit.

## But They Need to Be Told What to Do!

Teenage girls often go through periods of distraction, where the simple techniques of organization elude them. They can't remember to take with them the homework they worked on until midnight. They can't remember to take the check you've carefully put out for them on the final day the payment for a school trip is due. They can't remember they've arranged to meet you so that you can drive them to the dentist—even if you had to leave work early to do so. They can't remember they promised to feed the neighbor's cat, and they certainly can't think things through: So they promise to baby-sit at six, but are not home from their basketball game until nearly seven o'clock.

Mothers provide background reminders, which become a backup system of a teen's memory. The necessary check is ready and set out on the counter; the shopping has been done for the lunch preparation; she has reminded her about the dentist appointment. Then her daughter complains, "You're always telling me what to do!" Suddenly, a mother's reminders are labeled "orders," and a mother herself is a nuisance. So a mother stands back. The daughter then forgets, and her forgetfulness isn't just inconvenient; it arouses a mother's concern (She's irresponsible/She reflects badly on me/She doesn't take in what I tell her). So a mother resumes her reminders and instructions, and the daughter again feels

that her status as an independent person is challenged. She
is insulted that her mother thinks she is as disorganized as
she sometimes seems, so her mother backs off. The cycle of
argument and retreat continues.

## Improving the Choreography

Trial and error involves more misses than hits. Sometimes
we blame someone else, such as a difficult daughter, for our
errors. Sometimes we overlook our successes because they
seem unremarkable. One way of improving our steps is to
notice what we are doing when we hit the target and what
we are doing when we miss it.

- First, think about what happened during a recent fight or
  tiff with a daughter. Try to identify the status issue in that
  conflict. Can you find a way of conferring status on her
  even as you continue to argue about unavoidable issues?
  Could you perhaps endorse her point of view, or ask her
  help, or show respect for her anger, even if it is directed
  at you?
- Reward your daughter when she gives way to your claim
  for status. She may do this by offering help, or following
  an instruction, or being nice to her little brother, or writing a thank-you note you've been bugging her about.
  Thanking her gives the message: "No one made you do
  this." In that way, her status is not compromised.

Mothers often describe dealing with a teenage daughter as "exhausting." There are many reasons: First, there
is maternal fear and protectiveness versus the demand for
independence; then, there is the tact needed to keep the
peace; there are attacks and accusations that zoom from

unexpected directions; there is the challenge of keeping track of activities and whereabouts and friends; and, throughout, there is uncertainty as to when and how much to trust. Alongside these large themes are the constant negotiations over status, negotiations that are barely named as quarrels, but which exhaust one's energy and tax one's sanity. Once one can identify them, and find one's way around them, they become highly rewarding exercises in keeping the relationship fresh and strong.

# 6.

## *Portraits of Mother/Daughter Meltdown*

**SOME QUARRELS LEAD** to greater understanding. In the midst of a routine discussion about the day's plans, your daughter shouts, "No, I hate going there!" or you ask a casual question about a friend, and tears suddenly well up in your daughter's eyes as she insists, "I don't want to talk about it!" You realize that an activity she once enjoyed is now a chore. You back off one line of conversation, but take note of new troubles in your daughter's life.

Sometimes, through bad temper, we learn that patterns of interaction we took for granted are no longer acceptable. A mother does something she has done a thousand times before, such as stroke her daughter's cheek or give her a good-morning hug, and suddenly she has committed a crime. The daughter uses bad temper to say, "I've changed." A spurt of temper sometimes arises from a sense of one's own lack of power. A daughter may raise her voice for emphasis because she feels that, otherwise, she won't be heard—only to realize that her impact is greater than she anticipated, and that she has, perhaps, toppled a conversation she would like to continue.

Losing one's temper can be a way of communicating how we feel. It is usually a clumsy strategy for making ourselves heard, when we are afraid no one is listening. When we expect responsiveness, we communicate more clearly and effectively, using other means of communication. Once a girl is assured that she will be able to correct and counter her mother's views simply by speaking up, she will not have to shout.

Quarrels are attempts to get things right, but sometimes quarrels cloud rather than clear the air. Sometimes we get stuck in patterns of conflict that go nowhere, solve nothing, and make things worse. Instead of moving closer, each digs herself deeper into an opposing position. There is war, not resolution.

Why do some quarrels escalate? Why do some mothers and daughters come together during a quarrel, whereas others, with an equal mix of love and goodwill, enter a state of meltdown? In this chapter we look at how really awful quarrels get started, why they tend to get worse, and what we can do to get things right.

## How One Small Conflict Goes Global

Here is one mother/daughter quarrel, emerging as many such quarrels do within a conversation that is meant to be friendly, but in which each then rushes to fan the flames to meltdown.

It is Saturday. Bridget has some work papers spread out on the kitchen table. Her fifteen-year-old daughter, Cassie, is preparing to go to the beach with friends. Twenty minutes earlier mother and daughter successfully concluded somewhat jittery negotiations about the time Cassie is due to return, whether her estimate of that timing is reasonable, how many people will be riding in the car, and who is driving. Both Cassie and Bridget said they were satisfied with the outcome. Cassie takes one last look at herself in the hall mirror. As she is smoothing down her eyebrows, Bridget steps into the hall.

Bridget: "All set?"

Cassie: "Yeah. Like my new sunglasses?"

Bridget: "They're gorgeous."

Cassie grins, swings one hip to the side, and poses in front of the mirror.

Cassie: "I can look right into the sun without even squinting."

Bridget: "You shouldn't look right at the sun! Not even in good sunglasses."

Cassie: "I know! I can look around in sunlight without squinting."

Bridget: "But you know you should never look straight at the sun?"

Cassie: "I KNOW THAT! Any five-year-old knows that!"

Bridget: "Don't you shout at me!"

Cassie: "Don't shout at *me*!"

Bridget: "I can't tolerate this. I get nothing but disrespect from you, nothing but lip."

Cassie: "You think I am the stupidest thing that ever walked this earth. You think I don't know anything. *You* don't know anything."

Bridget: "I'll tell you what I know. I know you're not going out today. I know you're grounded. I know you're going to your room right this minute."

Cassie pales, clearly shaken.

Cassie: "I have to meet people in a few minutes. Mom! I have to meet these guys."

Bridget: "In a few minutes you'll be in your room doing your homework."

Cassie: "I said I'd do it tomorrow. You said it was okay."

Bridget: "And now it's not okay. Get to your room."

Cassie: "NO!"

Bridget: "GET TO YOUR ROOM!"

Cassie, crying with rage: "I HATE YOU!" She half reaches for the outer door to the apartment, but Bridget grabs her wrist.

Bridget: "GET TO YOUR ROOM!"

This argument arises out of nothing, yet big issues and passionate feelings are at stake. Cassie begins in a positive way: She wants her mother to share her pleasure with her appearance. Her new sunglasses not only look good but are useful: She can look out on a sunny day and not squint.

When Bridget warns her daughter against the dangers of looking directly at the sun, her tone changes. Taking a protective position, she goes into maternal lecture mode. This sudden change in status upsets Cassie. The warning Bridget gives is irritating because it is unnecessary: Cassie knows she's not supposed to look directly into the sun. To remind her is to treat her like someone younger than five years old, and that's an insult. Her mother should know that she is a wise fifteen-year-old, but it seems that her mother forgets.

This is the inciting incident of the quarrel. Cassie then defends herself against her mother's insulting assumption that she needs to be told something she has known since she was five. In the heat of her defense, she shouts, and then her mother reprimands her for shouting. The issue then is: How do I deserve to be treated, and how do you treat me? Bridget, hurt by Cassie's shouting, sees not just one outburst but typical behavior ("I get nothing but disrespect from you"). Bridget says that this current argument is a continuing argument. The mother and daughter are no longer facing a single issue; the issue is now the quality of their relationship.

Cassie is outraged, but she does not defend herself against this charge. Instead, she goes back to her previous complaint that her mother does not appreciate how much she knows. She matches her mother's tactics of generalizing the offense she is currently committing. "You think I am the stupidest thing that ever walked this earth!" she accuses. For her, that is the crime; for her mother, it is the shouting, the disrespect, and, while this is not explicitly mentioned, lack of love. When, in the small pause following this accusation she sees her mother is unrelenting, she hurls another accusation: It is the mother who knows nothing.

According to teen logic, evidence of what her mother does not know about her is evidence of overall ignorance. On one level, this is grossly unfair; but in Cassie's eyes, the most important knowledge her mother should have is about her, and her mother does not seem to have that knowledge, so her mother's ignorance is significant, and leads to a statement of utter rejection.

Bridget then punishes Cassie by using her power as a mother to cancel the outing Cassie has planned. Utterly humiliated by her role as a naughty child, and deprived of a shared experience with friends, she loses all footing in the argument. Cassie is at the point at which she will walk out the door of the apartment rather than into her room, as her mother orders, at which point the mother/daughter relationship will be in meltdown.

## Common Steps to Meltdown

Sometimes a quarrel is ignited because our bodies are tuned to aggression. We may think we are calm because an issue has been sorted in our minds, but the physiological aftereffects of a previous conflict have not subsided. Bridget and Cassie both believe that the moderately tense conversation that took place fifteen minutes before ("When will you be home?" "How many people will be riding in the car?" "Who's the driver?") is at an end. Yet both Bridget and Cassie are still under stress. It takes much longer to calm down than many of us think. When our heart rates and adrenaline are still high, our anger is ignited much more easily than when we start out calm.

The second part of this conflagration is about status and love. Bridget's understanding of what Cassie is doing when she shouts plays a part in this meltdown. Bridget hears Cassie's cry "I know that!" as a rejection, when it is actually a plea for recognition ("Don't you see how much I know?"). Cassie is saying, "Take a new look at me" while Bridget hears, "Get away from me."

On Cassie's part, she wants her mother to join in the excitement of the prospective outing. Instead, her mother crushes her expectations. She faces humiliation with her friends at having to let them down, and she is utterly wrongfooted in her attempt to stand beside her mother as a friend.

Another pattern Bridget and Cassie use in their conflict that is more likely to lead to free fall than resolution is universalizing. Turning specific behavior into a global accusation turns up the heat. Bridget sees her daughter's protest as something that goes on all the time, and then Cassie follows this globalizing tactic. This tactic turns something happening now into something that is always happening. As a result, the problem seems enormous, and far too large to be solved simply by negotiating the issue at hand.

## Giving Up on an Argument Can Intensify the Quarrel

Sometimes a mother or daughter declares that there is no point in arguing. This withdrawal actually intensifies hostility; it implies that someone is not worth talking to, is "too stupid" or "dense" to understand, is "hopeless" or "useless." One variation of this common strategy occurs in the following quarrel:

Judith's fourteen-year-old daughter, Kirsty, comes into the kitchen for breakfast.

Judith: "How 'bout some toast?"
Kirsty: "Toast! That is a stupid suggestion."
After a pause, Kirsty mutters, barely audible: "You are really stupid."
Judith: "Get your own breakfast."
Kirsty: "I never eat toast."
Judith: "Fine."
Kirsty: "I always get my own breakfast anyway. And you know I don't like talking the first thing in the morning."
Judith: "Fine."
Kirsty: (mimics) "'Fine.'"
Judith: "There's no point in talking to you. (pause) Is there?"
Kirsty: "Well—there's no point in talking to you. All you want is some sweet little kid. 'Where's a smile for your mom?' It drives me nuts."
Judith walks out of the kitchen. Kirsty kicks a chair.

Judith's take is that her daughter is "impossible," but she misses the move her daughter makes to repair the argument and to state her overall point. On the face of it, Kirsty is totally unreasonable. Judith makes a neutral suggestion about what to eat. Kirsty sees this as a sign of her mother's stupidity. Judith experiences her daughter's morning grumpiness as a personal rejection, and she responds in kind with a cold "Fine." When Kirsty challenges this move to close the conversation through mimicry, her mother makes another, more wounding, closure ("There's no point in talking to you"), Kirsty makes the obvious rejoinder ("Well, there's no point in talking to you"), but she goes on to explain what it is that has annoyed her in her mother's suggestion that she have toast. She does not like to be "babied"; she resents the assumption that she will smile sweetly at her mother. She is, in effect, explaining that the question whether she wants toast seems to belittle her, to assume that she's a kid who needs Mom to get her breakfast. Kirsty offers an oblique apology ("And you know I don't like talking the first thing in the morning,"), which her mother ignores, because she simply hears the rejection. Judith ends things coldly by walking silently out of the kitchen, and it is her mother's failure to take her point ("I don't like being treated like a kid because now I feel older") that frustrates Kirsty, who then kicks a chair.

If Judith could avoid the meltdown technique of giving up on a person ("There's no point in talking to you"), if she saw the message Kirsty wanted to give her, rather than read the message of the stereotypical "impossible" teen, this spat would have a very different ending.

## *Predictable Meltdown Moves*

Communication is a system. We often see ourselves reacting to what others say and do, without realizing that their words and actions are in part reactions to ours. We may also forget that our words won't be the end of the matter, but will trigger more reactions. Sometimes we need to think about the effect our words are likely to have on someone else, more than whether we are justified in speaking them. Some things we say, however true, are bound to shut down negotiations.

Mothers and teenage daughters engage in constant negotiations about home management (cleaning up, preparing meals, caring for sibs, keeping noise at a reasonable level), about schoolwork, curfews, personal information, money, and moods. Lots of mother/daughter talk time is devoted to persuasion: "Will you do this?" or "Will you let me do that?" Often a simple expression of wish or need, a logical argument, or a request is enough to get a daughter to wash the dishes, clean up her room, turn down the music, do her homework, or come home at the right time. But in some families, and probably in all families some of the time, people get others to do things by nagging, yelling, or throwing tantrums. Using unpleasant behavior to get what you want is called *coercion*.[1]

Coercion involves glares and grimaces and scowls, whining, mockery, mimicry, sarcasm, threats, coldness, humiliation, shouting, slamming, and breaking. It involves shrugging gestures, which indicate: "Get away from me," "Don't bug me," "Don't touch me," "I can't stand it that you're near me," as well as silence and feigned nonchalance.

Parents revert to coercion because they are at their wits' end. They do not have the power over a teen that they do over a child. They no longer have the edge that greater physical strength once gave them, and their teenager may no longer respond to emotional controls, such as parental disapproval, disappointment, or anger. A teen may be looking a few years down the road, when, in her imagination, she will "be free of my mom forever," while a parent is looking at ways to ensure her daughter's survival until she is ready to be free. In desperation, a parent tries to control situations by casting derision on a teen.

Common coercive remarks include:

"Just do what you're told!"
"Leave me alone!"
"Can't you show some respect?"
"Just who do you think you are?"
"Are you crazy?"
"You must think I was born yesterday."
"What's the matter with you?"

Then there are familiar global accusations and complaints:

"Your attitude stinks."
"You never do what I ask."
"I have to nag you to do anything."
"I'm sick and tired of hearing you talk to me like that."

The impact of hostile comments and commands is torturous. Pain is inflicted at increasing intervals until someone gives in. Teen and parent both escalate their efforts to inflict pain as they coerce the other person into submission. Each learns that the way to win an argument is to inflict the most pain on the other. When teen and parent fall into that pattern, both lose the argument.

## Volume Control: Why Shouting Hurts

Many mothers say they shout because a daughter makes them shout. They want to be nice, but a daughter's behavior defeats this wish. Yet in yelling they are using pain control. They are also encouraging the daughter to use pain control. Shouting or raising voice volume turns up the heat. Shouting meets with a shouted response.

Being shouted at is awful. We respond to shouting as though to a physical danger. A child frequently cries when a mother shouts, even if she is shouting at someone or something else. A mother may be fuming at a torn contact lens, or at the fact that she can't find her briefcase, but a very young child will nonetheless feel that she herself is under threat. Shouting stimulates a primitive panic, with fears of danger and abandonment.

An older child is likely to be irritated by a mother's tirade, over a broken dishwasher or stalled car, for example. She will be angry because her mother's anger triggers a rush of adrenaline: "Why should I be jolted into physical alert just because my mom's out of control?" she demands. She can key into the reality that there is no physical danger, but she cannot send this message to her body. The elemental panic she experienced as an infant and child stays with her.

For a mother, the daughter's shouting also has primitive reverberations. A baby's cry is pitched just right to get a parent's full attention, and to gear her to do whatever she can to stop it. Usually, a parent puts a stop to these cries by giving her baby what the baby wants: food, holding, warmth. Sometimes, she despairs because she cannot soothe the baby. She may read the cries as an accusation of her mothering skills, and become angry herself.

Children's cries and tantrums continue to have enormous power over their parents. The screaming toddler at the grocery checkout raises a mother's blood pressure and heart rate. She begins to perspire and experience an overall sense of dread. A child's whining in a toy store ("I want that. Buy that. Please. Buy that. I want that. Please. PLEASE!") can bring a parent to panic level, with the threat of her child's tantrum and displeasure as keenly felt as that of physical danger.

"Stop whining," "Don't coax," "You're a spoiled brat" are some of the things a parent may say to put a stop to behavior aptly labeled "pester power." While the best tactic is a calm broken-record approach, with an unheated version of "no" repeated at each request, a more usual and instinctive response is to escalate the volume of one's own voice to match the painful pitch of a child's cries, until the anger of one breaks down the other. Each uses coercion, and each tries to top the pain control used by the other. Each sees increased coercion as the best strategy to win an argument.

## Pestering

One of the most common forms of coercion used by teens is to pester. This is practiced by whining children, but it is sharpened and refined by teens. Pester power does not just consist of pleading or whining. It is a series of threats to make your life miserable if you don't give in. Sometimes the response is to issue a counterthreat. But as the teen is fighting for what she sees as her life, and the mother is fighting to preserve both her teen's safety and her own peace and quiet, neither is likely to give in gracefully.

"I dread arguments," Judith says, referring to Kirsty's skill at using pestering to achieve a result. "She'll ask whether she can go to this club, and then I'll start asking about the details, and there are more and more reasons why I have to say 'no': Some friend's boyfriend whom I never set eyes on is driving; the club closes at two o'clock in the morning, or maybe three, so I know I have to say 'no' and I know saying 'no' is going to be hell. Even her little sister can't stand it. She says, 'Not this again!' and runs upstairs. And [my partner] only has to come in the door to smell the problem. He tries to make light of it, and calls it common teen stuff, but it makes me feel awful.

"Kirsty is relentless. If I tell her she can't do something, she refuses to accept it. She'll go on and on. She'll sulk, and argue, and tell me she'll never have any fun as long as I'm her mother. And even when I get to the point where I think it's settled and she understands she's not going, she'll start on another tack, and try to reason with me, and then get furious because I won't listen to what she thinks of as reason. Half the time it turns out that other parents aren't letting their daughters do this stuff either, so it turns out I don't look like the worst parent in the world after all. But that doesn't make any difference. The next time is just as bad, and we have to go through the same thing again. She is so— Oh, the way she punishes me. When it starts, I really wish I could just run away and hide. If my fear weren't even worse than the fights, I'd just say 'yes' immediately."

Instead of saying "yes" immediately, Judith makes a brutal bid for authority: "Don't you dare talk to me like that" or "Don't even think of leaving this house." And so, the parent issues orders, and the teenager retaliates with pain control, and arguments escalate rather than get resolved.

## Why Keeping Our Cool Can Be So Difficult

One thing that terrorizes mothers as a daughter places herself in an opposing camp is concern about what she might do to herself. Opposition to a mother can lead to lawlessness: ("I'm not going to listen to you." "I'm going to do whatever I want." "You can't stop me."). It can lead to recklessness ("I want to do all the things my mother forbids"). It can lead to self-destructiveness ("Getting badly hurt is the best way to hurt my mother").

But there is another side to the extreme unease we feel when we are under attack by a teenage daughter. Memory of battles with our own mother can haunt us as we battle with our daughter. "I thought my mother was useless. I thought I would never be like her. And I'm not. Really, I'm not. Becky can say things to me I could never say to my mother. I'm younger—not in years, but I'm younger mentally—than my mother was, and there's just not the same kind of generation gap between me and Becky that there was between my mother and me. But there's still this awful stuff that gets between us and she ends up sounding just like I sounded when I was fourteen, and I guess I end up sounding like my mother. I hate it! I just hate it!"

When women reflect on motherhood, they do so in two very different modes. The first mode, as mothers themselves, is full of compassion, hope, and understanding. As mothers themselves, women highlight an overpowering love, informed by willingness to take on any burden for the sake of their children. The second mode, as daughters of mothers, often signals a harsh shift to complaint and accusation: about what her mother would not understand, what she refused to see, what she wanted for herself, what she denied her daughter. Listening to the voices of women speak in these two modes, you can hear the pitch and rhythm of voices change. In the first mode, there are longer phrases, voices are pitched lower, softer; there are more pauses, receptive to reply. In the second mode, as women speak of their own mothers, voices are brittle, phrases are short, declamatory, uninviting, as though to say "I don't want to be told that things were different. I may sound unfair, but I'm not. You don't know my mother."

It is possible to live with this double view of motherhood until one's daughter hits adolescence, and the first mode clashes with the second. "Am I as bad as she was?" is a question that often shoots through mother/daughter conflict. Many women say that a motive for maintaining a good relationship with their teenage daughters is to avoid being like their own mothers; they try to prevent their own daughters from feeling toward them the way they felt toward their mothers when they were teenagers. Then, in a heated interchange, a woman hears her mother in her own voice, saying the very words, using the same phrases her mother used against her. She feels her own former anger and outrage flare up in her daughter's heart, against her. Suddenly, the two divergent views of motherhood clash: one of compassion and value, as a mother focuses on her child, and one of opposition and ridicule, as a daughter judges her mother. She feels herself to be the loving mother, friend, confidante, and mentor to her daughter; she sees herself as the rigid, overprotective, controlling, and inhibiting mother who doesn't understand, won't listen, and just can't see. She feels "forced" into a role that she does not feel belongs to her. It isn't simply her daughter who is a stranger; the daughter threatens to turn the mother into a monster whose love is useless. Self-doubt increases a mother's anger, and she may blame her daughter for triggering this unease.

## Why Each Blames the Other

People are not naturally skilled observers of their own behavior. Since many quarrels between daughter and mother involve angry and irritable suppositions about what each is doing to the other, the arguments are characterized by hypercriticism and by subsequent brooding on mutual injustices.

A mother feels that the daughter instigated the quarrel. She showed disrespect; she expressed unprovoked annoyance; she refused to listen to her (do what she said, acknowledge what she said, follow her advice). A mother knows she is shouting, but she will often say she had no choice, that her daughter made her do it.

The daughter is convinced that the fault lies with the mother. She is being unreasonable. She is spoiling her fun. She is making a mountain out of a molehill.

Most mothers come to realize, as they live with adolescent girls, that their daughters exaggerate whatever they see as a maternal flaw. "You never let me do anything I want to do," or "You don't want me to be happy," or "You never care what I want!" or "You have no respect for my judgment" they declare, overlooking most of what their mother actually does allow her daughter to do. Mothers are far less aware of their own tendency to misrepresent a child's behavior. When mothers were asked to estimate how often a child coaxed, nagged, or whined, they were found to overestimate this by a factor of 600 percent.[2]

Mothers may idealize their beloved children, but they also exaggerate their flaws: "Why do you always have to make things so difficult?" and "What can't you ever listen to a word I say?" or "You never get home on time!" are remarks that show, at the moment she is speaking, that a mother takes a negative perspective as the complete picture. In her anger and frustration, she is stereotyping the daughter. For a teen who is trying, however clumsily, to gain her mother's recognition of her new and future self, this maneuver feels like a slap in the face.

The tragedy is that each person in this conflict believes her feelings to be basically good. Each wants to maintain the attachment. Yet each, at times, stereotypes and diminishes the other. Each feels the other is being unfair to her. Each is right. But being right is not enough. When we understand what a daughter is aiming at in her "unfair" behavior, we can respond more effectively.

When a daughter shows irritation at what a mother says or tells her to do, a mother's critical response is likely to be:

"She has a bad attitude."

"She has no respect."

Her practical response is:

"I do not have the power to control or protect her. I must find some way of controlling her in order to protect her."

Her emotive response is then likely to be:

"She does not love me."

"She is rejecting me."

A more productive response might be:

"What I have just said is irritating her now."

"I have to explain the dangers in various situations as they arise."

"She needs me to acknowledge her views."

"She needs me to trust her judgment."

Understanding plays a crucial role in interpreting what is going on around us. When we see that a daughter's criticisms or angry outbursts are not gestures of rejection, we can begin to respond more effectively. After all, we are pulled into this sucker's game because she trusts us, eventually, to come up with the right response, and the "right" response involves switching off the meltdown track and onto one moving toward recognition and validation.

A daughter argues heatedly because she wants her mother to see her point, even if she does not agree with her. It would not occur to her to keep her criticisms of her mother to herself, for her criticisms lack punch and purpose if a mother does not confirm them in some way. At the very least, she should be angered or hurt by them.

Sometimes a girl's anger is so vehement because she believes it is ineffective. Her mother seems unchanging, implacable, strong, sure. When she comes up against a stereotype of herself, she feels humiliated and frustrated.

Equally, a mother may use far more force than necessary in argument because she too feels that she is not getting through. She is not aware that her voice reverberates through her daughter with a physical force. She is not aware that her daughter shouts, in part, to make her own voice louder than her mother's, and that she screams sometimes in protest at the depths to which her mother's voice and presence reach within a daughter.

## What We Can Do

To improve our relationships we have to take a cold look at what we ourselves do. When we shout, we blame our daughters. But blame doesn't help. We can track our own responses, perhaps even tape what we say. How often do we make a coercive move, twist a rhetorical question in like a knife, dismiss a daughter's defense or excuse.

- We can avoid arguing about her "attitude" or her "lack of respect" when discussing an issue. Let her walk out of the room. Let her make a face and slam the door. She then has some control over the pace of the discussion, and she can take a break. She may be leaving the scene of the discussion as a means of controlling her display of anger. It's not a crime, and it's not a sign that she hates or disrespects her mother. She feels that her resistance and opposition are small next to (what she sees as) your certainty. She thinks her power is less than yours. Your voice, inside her head, is very loud, magnified by years of childhood dependence and love. So she may shout it down, even as you are quiet and reasonable. From her point of view, she is matching your tone.
- Don't try to repair things while you're still angry. Physiologically, you are still in a state of anger, and your temper will be likely to flare up again when your planned peace proceedings reach a hitch.
- The experience of teenage rage, both for the parent and the teen, is traumatic. Repair work is never so necessary as after an awful fight. How this postquarrel rage is handled is critical to the repair of the relationship. It can wait until you are both calm.
- When you talk about what happened, avoid a thorough debriefing. Sidestep the insults she cast on you and the ones you may have cast on her. She will probably be shaken and humiliated by her own loss of control. Try to

reconnect rather than refocus on the details of what was said during the battle.

- Keep your voice low—don't shout; she'll hear the anger and nothing else. Hand movements can also seem aggressive (especially if they are directed toward her, such as finger shaking, or pointing), and they raise the temperature of the discussion. Keep them at a minimum.

- Don't think of repair work as proving a point or getting even. Don't think of an apology as giving in. "I'm sorry you're upset" is different from "I'm sorry; I was wrong."

- When she seems calm, you can try subtle physical closeness: If you can't cuddle or touch, keep close, but avoid touching her, and if she squirms or shudders, step away. Think of how many times you've been told "Get out of my space."

- When she is honest and open, reward her. Sometimes the best reward is to take in what she says and say something like "I'm glad you said that."

To put damage control on an ongoing fight:

- Explain your anger in terms of your own feelings: You are either concerned about her safety, or her schoolwork, or you need her to show consideration for others, or responsibility. Focus on these rather than on her general character, attitude, or values.

- If she does threaten to terrorize you, stop the argument, but don't pose counterthreats. "You do that, and I'll come down on you like a ton of bricks"/"You do that, and you'll wish you'd never been born"/or even "You do that, and you'll be sorry" are examples of pain control and lead to escalation.

## Repair Mechanisms

We can stall a fight when we pick up on a daughter's efforts to repair a rift. Repair mechanisms are any of a number of attempts to reach out to someone before the quarrel becomes too negative.

A repair attempt can be a reminder of positive feelings. Many mother/daughter quarrels end with a compliment: Amy breaks her mother's angry silence by saying "I like the way you're wearing that scarf." Mary turns from a fight with her mother to focus on the family Labrador: "Look at Sally's ears. She doesn't like the sounds we're making." Gina rolls her eyes to the ceiling and asks, "Can you be any more annoying than that?" and her mother accepts this glimmer of humor by answering, "Oh, I think I might be able to manage it."

A repair mechanism can also involve making a concession. This can involve negotiation ("You can pick me up from the party if you don't come inside and let me meet you at the corner") or acknowledgment of a point of view. Teenagers are unfairly stereotyped as unconcerned with maintaining relational harmony. As mothers learn how to recognize teens' often minute and oblique peace offerings, they can make good use of a daughter's wish to influence the relationship.

## When to Get Help Rather Than Giving Up

No mother can solve every problem a daughter throws at her. Persistent and vicious quarrels may require repair work of someone outside the family, someone who can mediate with some emotional distance. Sometimes a daughter is in such distress that she cannot respond positively to anyone as closely bound to her as her mother is.

Questions that could help assess whether the mother/daughter relationship is in need of expert repair would include:

- Does every conversation of substance end in a heated argument?
- Do you dread talking to your daughter?
- Do you feel that your daughter is always lying to you?
- Do you find quarrels getting worse and worse?
- Is it increasingly difficult to resolve a disagreement in discussion?

Mothers and daughters continue to quarrel because neither gives up on the other. Sometimes we need to go outside the family to seek advice about regulating the tactics we use in the heated debates and negotiations with a daughter. Underlying the continuing quarrels is the hope that needs will be met. The arguments will continue for better and for worse, throughout a daughter's life, until these needs are met.

# 7. Learning to Fight: Friendship and Conflict

"**IF ANGE** and I could be friends, I think my greatest goal would be fulfilled."

A mother's common wish is to be her daughter's friend. While many women say it was impossible for them, as teens, to be friends with their mothers, they count on better luck forging a friendship with their own teenage daughters.

"There's not the same generation gap between me and Ange. There was a real opening up of ideas during my teens, and my mother and I stood on opposite banks. Sex, marriage, children, career, length of skirt, eye makeup—you name it, we disagreed so violently that discussion was pointless. I don't think Ange thinks I speak a different language."

As a teenager and young adult, Pippa joined the cult of youth and learned to identify herself "as young, not old, and that self-image is still with me." She, like many mothers in my study, has participated in the social changes that have an impact on her own daughter's future. She bridled against her mother's traditional expectations about a woman's place in the home and her mother's notions of sexual purity. She has encouraged her own daughter to develop a range of abilities, to speak out and to go for what she wants.

The mothers in my study frequently said say that they felt closer to their daughters' generation than to their mothers'. They had clear memories of their own teenage years, and though they said they "had changed a lot since then," they felt they were "basically the same person." They expected to be able to identify with a daughter.

Many also said that they were going through a parallel phase of development. As daughters move through their teens, mothers feel that they are assessing a different kind of future for themselves. Anticipating fewer family demands and experiencing an increase in physical energy, Pippa now looks forward to being "more my own person, and developing lots of things I haven't had time for." While her own mother had been "at a loss when she realized I was growing up and actually said when I left home that she was staring at a dead end," Pippa sees her daughter's increasing independence as an opportunity for new personal freedom. "At my age my mother was old. I feel younger now than I did at thirty."

As she speaks, she catches sight of the comic side: "As a teen I saw my forty-year-old mom as old, but now I am forty, that doesn't seem old." But she insists that there are real changes, above and beyond the inevitable change in perspective as to what counts as "old." She gives clear examples of things that divided her and her mother, but that do not divide her and Ange.

"My mother thought I had every material thing a body could want. Whenever I asked for something, she'd throw up her hands and ask God to have mercy on this spoiled child. She said I had more clothes and toys and books and records than her imagination could have conjured when she was my age. Half the time she was proud of this, but the other half she worried it would affect my character. She worried that I'd grow up without learning the value of money. She worried that I'd be irresponsible, and so on. I know my daughter has a lot more gadgets than I had, but I don't think her life will be materially easier on the whole, and she's not in danger of becoming a little princess, no matter how many nice shoes she has, because she'll have to work to earn a living, and she knows that."

Pippa continues to argue her case that she shares a lot with her daughter: "My daughter's clothes are different from mine, but not totally different. For my mother, fashion was something just foolish young girls cared about. There was no connection whatever on that level." And she returns to her empathy with her daughter's forward-looking concerns: "I still have a future, both personally and professionally. That's as exciting to me as my daughter's future is to her." Pippa also feels that, like her daughter, she is at a phase of rapid learning: "It's easier to take on new things. I can develop skills that utterly defeated me in my twenties. We really do have a lot in common."

On a good day, mothers say that the hierarchical aspect of parenthood has been eroded. They want to be a confidante and friend rather than an authority figure; yet, inevitably, they shout and command, because the alternative of letting a daughter go her own way, unguided, can be terrifying. Pippa says she feels "awful and unsettled" when she has to lay down the law to Ange. "I feel I've violated that ideal. And I sound just like my mother." Like so many mothers, she registers a split between her ideal of mother as friend and the reality of mother as disciplinarian and guardian.

The ideal of being a friend to one's daughter comes up against three things: the ineradicable position of mother, the false ideal many girls and women hold of friendship, and the need for daughters and mothers to be open to one another in ways in which conflict is inevitable. In this chapter I will look at the ways in which mother/daughter friendships are sometimes countered by the need to retain parental authority, and how girls can learn how to manage peer conflict by the experience of intimate and fertile conflict with a mother.

## New Quarrels and Old Quarrels

Mother and daughter quarrels begin in earnest just at the time when girls themselves grapple with the intricacies of conflict with girlfriends. Conflicts with peers are often hidden and indirect.[1] They are more likely to take place behind one's back than face-to-face. The shape of these quarrels among girls who are close, and who, a day before, may have considered each other a "best friend," is familiar to mothers who experienced it themselves, and may still scrape its edge as they fall out with female friends or colleagues.

Mothers of adolescent girls often dread the advent of the friendship wars. "Uh-oh, here it is," they may think as they see their daughter come home crying from school for the first time because another girl called her "a name." Most mothers don't want to remember the pain of those years, so they try to minimize it for their daughter. "So what?" they say. "What do you care what she says? Don't let it bother you." Yet as mothers, we often find ourselves quite helpless in this situation. It may be one of the first signs that we cannot control the world for our growing daughters. Among our own friends, we may ask, "What should I do when my daughter is not invited to the party she thinks everyone else has been invited to?" or "What do I do if my daughter chooses girls who I think are pressuring her into doing bad things?" These dilemmas occupy mothers of teenage girls as they see their daughters pass through the threshing floor of friendship.[2]

The last thing girls want is for a mother to interfere. "Stay out of it!" Ellie, twelve, tells her mother, Ruth. "You don't understand. You'll only make things worse." Only someone her own age, she believes, can understand the complex rules that operate in girls' friendships. But mothers do understand these rules, and can help a daughter survive them by teaching her that face-to-face conflict does not destroy a relationship.

## Rules of Engagement

One of the hardest things in any relationship is learning how to disagree—how to fight as freely as very young children, and make up as readily. At times, however, walls spring up and chasms open that may be or seem untraversable. Girls sometimes confront one another outright, but more likely, they will tiptoe around each other, burying their negative feelings in order to avoid open clashes and preserve the illusion of harmony.

In early adolescence, girls are simultaneously terrified and fascinated by the dynamics of confrontation. They discuss among themselves scenarios and procedures: "Should I say anything?" "Do you think she's really sorry?" "Can you believe what she said?" "What I should've said is . . ." They enact, reenact, brood, assess other girls' "crimes," and try to hone their own tactics. They ask what a good close relationship is, how people should be treated, what's right, what's fair, what's loyal. Their arguments reveal tensions about possessiveness and independence, questions about how each should be treated and how a girl should behave if the rules for fair treatment are broken.

Girls often battle with the concern that if one fights back, one is guilty of not being nice. The self-justifications ("I was mean to her because she was so awful") or the nagging self-doubt ("Was I mean to say that?") lend these conflicts their psychological power. Among their friends, girls are often bound by impossibly angelic ideals of who they should be and how they should treat others. Paradoxically, the ideals of femininity may prevent girls from getting close again. Because girls feel pressure to "be nice" to each other's face, harsh feelings fester. But few girls will risk being openly angry for fear of being called a bitch and losing others' regard in consequence. Those who do show their anger may offend a friend so much that reconciliation becomes impossible.

Because of the unease girls and women feel when they experience conflict with someone they love, they tend, when things go wrong, to search for an explanation. "What happened?" and "Whose fault is it?" mothers and daughters ask themselves and one another, trying, in retrospect, to put the pieces together again. Often fights arise as each tries to understand a previous quarrel. They air complaints and countercomplaints. This sometimes leads to understanding. It sometimes leads to another quarrel.

The difficulty teenage girls have negotiating conflict with their girlfriends, and working around the constraints of

being a "good friend" (every bit as demanding as the constraints imposed by the ideal of "the good wife"), can be
eased by learning about the perks of conflict. They can learn
through a mother's open reflections on the meaning of conflict in their lives.

The rules for talking to friends are tricky. Ellie can boast
to her mother about something clever she said, about an
improved time in track, about the effect of her hairstyle or
makeup, and her mother is delighted with the news; but
when she speaks in the same way to her friends she is
"showing off" or "thinks too much of herself," and her friends
work together to put her down. The pleasure of a success
drains away as she catches the whispered phrases, half
behind her back, half meant to be overheard or passed back
to her, about "thinking too much of herself" or "thinking
she's better than anyone else."

Her friends often reject her, perhaps arguing that they are
punishing her for her own good. It is cruelty hidden in the
guise of love: "I really think you should know this," or "I
really like you and that's why I want to tell you how much
you are annoying people and why people are talking about
you behind your back." While girls also gain self-confidence
and learn their way around the human world through their
friends, they, inevitably, go through rough times during
their teen years. On the one hand, the openness a mother
can offer is a reprieve. On the other hand, if girls have to
cover over their real thoughts with a mother as well, they
feel isolated.

At the same time a girl may work hardest to present only
a good or "cool" or whatever is acceptable face to her friends,
she becomes hypersensitive to her mother's hypocrisy. Alex
says of her mother, Vicky: "She says, 'You shouldn't care

what other people think of you,' and then she goes batty before she goes out. 'Am I wearing the right thing? Can I face all those intimidating people? Can I keep up a conversation without looking stupid?' She goes on and on about stuff like this—and then says I shouldn't care what people think!"

This is a phase in which girls are likely to feel new pressures to conform. They begin to censor thoughts and feelings that do not fit in with their ideals of a "good girl." Of course, with their mothers, girls usually do not suffer from these constraints. "She's not afraid to give me a piece of her mind," "She doesn't spare my feelings," "She doesn't keep anything back from me," "She sure doesn't want to play the perfect girl when I'm at home," mothers remark.

This relational space to state their differences, show their opposition directly, face-to-face, and proclaim loudly, "This is who I am: Take me or leave me," and get the response "I see you and love you" offers a reprieve from the hidden culture of aggression.

## False Resolutions

The false ideal of a perfect friendship cannot be upheld between mother and daughter, because the ideal of friendship is a false one and demands false supports—the illusion, perhaps, that we always agree, or we are never angry, and that we never fight.

Mothers and teenage daughters who "never fight" are rare; and rarely are they happier or closer than mothers and teenage daughters who do quarrel. In avoiding quarrels, a mother and daughter may forgo getting to know each other. They may be "at peace" because they have given up on each other. More important than keeping the peace is fighting well. When girls under the age of eighteen told me they never fought, argued, or engaged in conflict with a mother, I asked, "How do you manage that?" The most common answer was "By lying."

It is disheartening how adept some teenagers get at lying. There are several different patterns of lying. The most common is strategic lying, lies, usually, about where she has been and where she is going. Some lies are small scale ("I told her I went to Kate's. Explaining that I was with this guy was going to be too heavy"). But for Senka, sixteen, lying becomes a staple feature of her relationship with her mother. "I do it automatically now. I think I lie even when I don't have to. The less she knows, the less flack I'll get. I tell her I'm with guys she likes, when I wouldn't really be caught dead with them. I make her think I'm all involved in this group science project, and that gives me a permission slip to hang out after school. I have to make a real decision to tell her the truth, like I decided to do when I got a job, because I knew she might come by the store sometimes."

For Senka, lying supplies her with a convenient mask that allows her to get along with her mother:

> Before, she was always on at me, and it went nowhere. Now she thinks I'm sweet. She thinks I've "matured nicely" over the past few months. She sees the facade. She believes in it totally, because she doesn't know anything else. I tell her I'm friends with girls I would never hang out with, but they're girls my mom would like the look of. So I get this big smile when I say I'm going to Claire's house, or Rachel's. And if she asks me something about my evening, I give her lots and lots of detail. It just all happens to be made up. What she doesn't know is that I just don't let her see me anymore.

While Senka is extreme in her use of strategic lying, more than half of the teenage girls in my study said they used strategic lying sometimes, to go where they wanted to, with whomever, and avoid argument.

Senka's mother, Jenny, is not as fooled as her daughter thinks, but does note the distance between them. "It started when she was thirteen, and went on until last year, when we went through a real bad patch. We were always fighting, and I was worn out. I didn't know how I would survive until she was out of the house. But gradually I guess we just worked things out. I try not to give her trouble, and she's trying too. The fights were awful, really. I thought they'd kill us both."

When conflict reaches an impasse and fights don't achieve the tasks they set out to achieve, girls take evasive action. They punish a parent by refusing to present her with the true self, and so they close off any bridge building.

Some girls say they do not have another viable option. "My mom doesn't give me a choice. If I'm going to have any life I have to lie. I'd never be able to do anything my friends do." Wei feels "really awful" when she lies, but that is "the only way I can do what my friends do and not miss out. I can't change my parents' values. They're set in their ways, and I can't make them see my case. I don't lie often, and I hate it, and it really affects whether I can have fun, but I'd hate not joining in on something even worse." And Meg lies to her father because, if he knew about her abortion, and realized she had had sex, "he would have a heart attack and die." These girls, using strategic lying to make things easier, fail to test their parents' responses and live with their imaginary extreme versions of a parent's response.

## The Protective Daughter:
## "I put on a happy face."

While strategic lying paves the way to short-term ease, placatory lying is more complicated. "Everything's fine with me and Noel" or "Nothing's wrong at school" when spoken as a lie, may protect a girl "from going into stuff that's too complicated or scary." Kath explains that she also feels her mother doesn't need to know about her "rotten love life and trouble at school. She has enough on her plate."

In placatory lying, girls paint a rosy picture of their inner and outer worlds as a way of removing pain from the relationship with a mother. Allison, fifteen, says, "I don't like bringing her all these downers. Mom gets so anxious when I'm upset. You know, she goes around trying to cheer me up. She sometimes buys me little junky presents—the sort of thing I used to get in my Christmas stocking, tacky jewelry or cute little candy. And then she keeps asking me how I am, like suddenly I'm going to give her the news that everything's okay."

Allison's mother, Sam, says, "When Allie's unhappy, I feel bad and I do whatever I can to make her feel better. It's hard to get over the 'Mommy will kiss it better' thing."

But for Allison, the matter goes deeper than that: "If I say something, you know, something about just some of these awful feelings I have—about myself, my friends—she gets this worried look and starts this string of regrets: 'We shouldn't have moved here.' 'We should have put you in a different school.' 'Do you want to think about changing schools now?' 'Would it help to see a therapist?' And I don't want to have to deal with all that as well as this, so when she says, 'Are things better?' I say, 'Yeah, things are much better.'

I don't feel any better. I probably feel worse, but I don't want to deal with her anxiety."

It is one thing to want a daughter to be happy, and another to feel so anxious when she is unhappy that we make it difficult for her to express that unhappiness. Sometimes when a mother sees she can't help her daughter, and feels that she should, she then feels herself to be powerless.

But teenagers inevitably experience some psychological pain. They sometimes cast it back at us, in an accusation out of the blue, or by general moodiness. "My daughter makes sure that she's never the only one who's unhappy," Bridget explains. "Cassie's determined that I'm going to suffer with her." Sometimes we are powerful simply by being the person whom a daughter can blame for her own unhappiness.

## Lies of Omission: "I can't bother my mother with this."

A girl who never fights or rarely fights with or criticizes her mother may avoid conflict because she feels it is more important to care for a mother's feelings than explore their differences or force new recognition from her.

Teenage girls are eager to get to know their mothers in new ways. They are proud of their increased capacity for understanding, empathy, and self expression. They are quick to resent reserve and disguise, quick to attack masks and hypocrisy. When they do see that a mother is, for whatever reason, reluctant to open up a genuine conversation, they search diligently for the right key, hoping that, this time, the ignition will fire.

In the course of this search, some girls discover that a

mother is too vulnerable to be open. She herself cannot admit what her problems are, how deep her fear or how helpless she feels in the face of her own weakness. Just at the time when girls need mothers to help them describe and recognize who they are, they may feel a panicky emptiness when a mother is not strong enough to put forth the effort to get to know them.

Jane, now sixteen, says that she has known "for a long time, maybe a couple of years, maybe forever" that her mother needs to be protected from her children's needs. "I must have realized before that she had these problems. At first I thought all mothers were like that. Then I saw they weren't. And then I got so embarrassed, you know, when she cried in front of my friends, or maybe screamed some. But now I understand that she really has a difficult time. Sometimes she cries. Sometimes she sleeps all day. Sometimes she gets angry and throws things, usually in the yard, usually just old dishes, things like that. I remember getting really mad at her myself, and saying 'Get it together, why don't you!' and now I feel bad about that, because she's the best mom, really, and I love her."

Jane sees that her mother is suffering from depression, and does what she can to protect her. By some measure, we would call her, and the many teens who are protective of a parent, "mature," and perhaps wish that our own daughters would be so considerate of us. But Jane's consideration is fueled by fear:

> I can't stand it when she falls apart. I never want to push her too far. Besides, I like being the strong one. Sometimes I'm terrified, but I don't show it. I just look her in the eye and say, "Mom, we can get through this."

Usually, when a girl sees a mother showing some signs of weakness, she goes in for the attack until her mother is roused to fight back. Daughters are prepared to force a mother out of apathy and into connection. But a mother who truly lacks the resources to speak out and state her true position forces her daughter to be protective.

Girls whose mothers have other debilitating problems, such as alcohol or drug addiction, also tend to be fiercely protective of them, and refuse to say "anything against her" because "she's doing her best" and "no one else can understand what she's up against." Indeed, mothers should receive criticism and complaint from daughters as a badge of their own perceived strength, and as proof that a daughter has not given up on them.

## Lying to Impress

Another disturbing pattern is anecdotal lying. Making things up, systematically and gratuitously, is usually a sign of deep dissatisfaction. This runaway lying is a sign that fabrications feel easier and safer than authenticity. Connie, fourteen, lies to her friends, and then has to lie to her mother to explain why their mothers express concern about her. She tells stories about personal crises—a series of visits to a doctor about a suspected ovarian tumor, which she periodically updates. She provides details of treatments and setbacks. She describes sympathetic doctors and cruel doctors. It is a long running story, and it is a lie.

Her mother is puzzled by questions from mothers of Connie's friends. "I hear you're having some trouble at home?" or "How is Connie?" and Sarah is confused, then angry and scared. "The school counselor said it was attention seeking and wanted to know about our home setup, and was I working full-time, and did we give Connie enough attention. How much attention does a kid need? We give her everything!"

Anecdotal lying can be compulsive, so that a girl lies knowing full well that she will subsequently be exposed. Yet she is unable, as Connie explains, "to keep from blurting it out." Connie makes up stories of being in an accident, and she relates its gruesome details in a phone conversation with a friend, knowing that on Monday, people will see she was not badly injured. "But at least for that moment, they're thinking, 'What a brave girl!'" She tells stories of amazing successes— she has been chosen for a part in Broadway play; just as she was walking in the mall, there was someone talent scouting. "Even if they think maybe it won't come about, they think for a minute at least, 'Gosh, she must be something.'"

The extent of problems here reach to the roots of a girl's sense of who she should be. Rarely can this syndrome be sorted out easily or quickly. Lying becomes a habit, often a compulsive one. But in most cases of false self-presentation, improved mother/daughter communication can challenge the assumption that lying is necessary to being admired or accepted. When mothers take the risk themselves of showing their daughters who they are and when they take the risk of admitting the ambiguities in their own lives, their daughters become open with them.

Jenny needs to show Senka that their fights won't "go nowhere forever." She needs to show that she can take knowledge of who her daughter is without throwing a fit.

Sam needs to stop taking the blame for Allison's unhappiness and instead let her talk about it her way. Learning to tolerate and bear painful feelings in ourselves and those we love is one of the most difficult trials of relationships. It is one thing to desire a daughter's happiness and another to deny her pain.

Sarah needs to let Connie speak of her shame at being who she is, and then assure her daughter that the mother sees her as the interesting person she will become.

## *Listening Practice*

Sometimes a daughter tries to say what she really thinks, but is silenced by a mother's shock or disapproval. "How dare you say that!" "You don't mean that!"

She may also feel silenced through a variety of more subtle ways. A parent who does not respond to what she says, or perhaps cuts off a conversation by interrupting or turning on the television or computer, undermines a daughter's efforts to focus her own thoughts.

If mothers become as sensitive to the adult tactics for silencing teens as their daughters already are, they can learn to listen. What they hear, in all probability, will not be so bad.

We can practice our ability to listen to the painful side of a daughter's life. Here is one exercise:

- Think of something that has happened to you in the past few months that has upset you. Talk to your daughter about this.
- Think of something about yourself you would rather your daughter did not know. It may be something significant from your past.

It's surprising how many daughters did not know that their mother had been divorced, or had had an abortion, or dropped out of college at one time, or had been sexually assaulted, or charged with shoplifting or drug possession. When we do not reveal these things, we seldom feel we are deliberately hiding something; in our view, we are simply not telling a daughter something that is, perhaps, none of her business, or that might upset her. But not telling creates a distance. Opening up exposes us, but it also brings us closer.

Teens work hard to shape a parent's view of them, to change a relationship that matters to them. Only in desperation, when the pain of maintaining the relationship outweighs their need for it, do they make a decision not to expose themselves to a mother. But even then, separation is never final. Girls never really give up on repairing a relationship with their mother; for a broken mother/daughter bond is a lifetime wound.

But girls do battle with an internal ideal of what they should be for their mother. If, for whatever reason, a mother finds conflict with a daughter intolerable, then a daughter, too, might decide to avoid conflict with a mother. In so doing, she loses out in one of the most important lessons of life: how to love and disagree; how to speak out without fear of damaging a relationship; how to insist that someone who loves you should really know you.

# 8.

# *My Mother, My Father: Two Different Relationships*

**AS FOURTEEN-YEAR-OLD MARY** explains why she trusts her mother with "things that are private and you don't want most people knowing about them," she says that her mother would "never laugh behind my back" or tell someone "who would use it against me." She reconsiders, however, noting that revealing private things to her mother does involve some risk: "She might tell my father. She does that sometimes, and it's not right, not if I've told her not to. But that's the worst thing she'd do, tell my father."

Whenever I present my work on mothers and daughters, I am asked: "What about daughters and fathers?" Sometimes, the question is posed by a father who feels left out of this dynamic story. Sometimes I am asked this by a father who feels that he, too, is involved in daily negotiations and tensions. Before continuing with mother/daughter stories, I here take time out to explore the ways that the father/daughter relationship dovetails with the mother/daughter plot.

Early on in my research on teenage girls' development I noticed that girls have a very different relationship with a mother and a father. Some girls said that their father was "the last person" they would go to for help with or discussion of a problem that caused embarrassment. The very idea of confiding in a father struck some girls as hilarious. "He'd be as uncomfortable as we would," Mary exclaimed. "Can you imagine having a heart-to-heart with Dad? About sex!" she demands of her sixteen-year-old sister, Louise.

Louise concurs: "He'd say, 'Yeah, yeah,' and squirm in his seat and change the subject."

"Or jump up to work in the yard," Mary added. "It would be a good way to get rid of him for hours."

Mary's responses to confiding in her father are closely linked to her expectation of what his feelings would be. She finds the prospect of speaking to him (about sex, or anything that embarrasses her) excruciating because her father, she imagines, would be out of his depth. If she chose him as a confidant, she would be casting him in a role he could not play. She elaborates:

"His eyes go all over the room when you start talking to him. It's as though I'm not there, as though all this"—and she looks down at her body, pulling her top against her chest—"hadn't happened." She looked at her sister for confirmation. Louise explains, "It's his way of being polite."

Together the sisters create a comic character: their inept dad.

Teenage girls have distinct and different relationships with their different parents. While most teenage girls describe a dynamic and intimate relationship with a mother, they frequently, in their initial words, say they do not "feel close" to a father. When I speak to daughters about their fathers, they reply with reference to their mothers.

"I can tell Mom that, but not my dad."

"It's easier to go shopping with my mom. It's hopeless with my dad."

"When only Mom is at home, we can just hang out and relax, and eat whenever we want. When Dad's around, it's like: He's home so we have supper at this time, and he wants to watch this channel, so we all have to."

## Sins of Omission

A researcher cannot get adequate information about a daughter's relationship with a parent—either its pleasures or its perils—through girls' accounts alone. To get a reasonably full picture, it is necessary to follow the micromoves of their conversations, and to put what a daughter says about her parent's capacity to understand and willingness to listen in a wider context. Some years ago, writing about teenage girls, I concluded that, during adolescence, daughters are not close to their fathers.[1] This perspective arose out of that imbalance I have already criticized when researchers base their conclusions about a relationship solely on what a girl says about her mother, and not what she says to her. One-dimensional information leads to one-dimensional conclusions.

Another lesson I learned in committing this bias to print—that teenage girls are not close to their fathers—is that girls are quick to complain about what parents do not do, see, or understand; but when they see their remarks in a relational context, they wish to reflect and revise their complaints. Seeing the impact of their anger or rejection on a mother stimulates their recognition that their words now have a different meaning from those spoken by a child. Girls, likewise, wished to revise what they had said about not being close to a father when they saw his response to this statement.

The material I had about teenage daughters and their fathers was limited, based as it was primarily on what girls say away from the heat of the relationship in action. But this omission in father/daughter material was difficult to fill. When I explained that I wanted to observe them together, teenage girl with father, the definition of "time together" was loose. In the time they spent together, they frequently were not in immediate verbal contact, but simply at home together. Whereas mothers and daughter will talk, no matter what else they happen to be doing together, a father can be "around" or "doing something with a daughter" but, in terms of interaction, remain very much in the background. It generally took twice as long to observe daughter and father interacting than mother and daughter, because even when father and daughter were together, there was less interaction between this pair.

## Who Adapts to Whom?

Teenage girls are proactive in getting their mothers to change. They are adept at signaling that it is time to update the relationship with them. With a father, they feel they have to be the one to adapt their expectations and impulses to his, in order to maintain a relationship. While fathers speak about their pleasure at being able to do more with a teenage daughter, and talk to her on a more adult level, they remain inflexible during conflict. The new engagement, set alongside this relational rigidity, creates contradictory feelings in many girls toward their fathers.

Naomi, fifteen, who is adept at negotiating changing status with her mother, initially insists, "I'm not that close to my dad." However, she reflects six months later, "I really do love my dad, and I like doing lots of things with him. There's something about the way he gets so involved. It's so serious. That's what makes it fun! And then sometimes, all of a sudden, he can hurt me so badly. We'll be doing something—yesterday we were putting up the tent to check we had all the bits for the trip next week—and suddenly I'm 'a pain in the neck' because I wasn't hammering in the spikes right, and he sent me off to do something else, like I'm a real failure."

These sudden reversals are common in parent/child relationships as cooperation crashes and interactions turn punitive. Whereas Naomi feels that even in anger her mother is able to focus on her feelings, she believes her father is locked in self-righteousness:

> He's not mad the way Mom would be. She can be nasty, but then she knows she's hurting me. To him, my feelings don't count—not while he's setting up that tent. Most of the time this doesn't matter, but when it comes, it's 'Wham!' like a slap in the face. And there's this lump of anger he just doesn't see, no matter what I say or do.

This teenage girl, concentrating on what a parent does or does not see, appreciate, or understand, is as offended by her father's conclusion that she is "a real failure" as she is by his ignorance of how and why his attitude hurts her. She has to weigh the fun of doing things with him against the frustrations. Once danger strikes, she can only lose her temper and walk away or brood angrily about parental crimes. ("I hate it when he does that. I sometimes feel—so, I don't know—violated.") She sees no point in engaging in the skillful choreography of negotiation with her father that she engages in with her mother:

I used to just cry when this sort of thing happened, and not really understand, I guess, why I felt so sad. Now it's still a shock, because so much of the time he's so much fun. But I clam up for a long time when this happens. And I'm not as forgiving as I used to be. I don't just forget.

She is guarded and careful with him for some time after such an episode. In withdrawing from her father, she is both protecting herself and punishing him. Though she does not believe that he "notices one way or another" when she disengages from him, she feels good about punishing him in this way. "It's a matter of my integrity," she explains. "I'm not going to talk to someone who treats me like that."

From her father's point of view, the episode is unimportant. "Oh, come on," he says as she continues to sulk. He does not understand the depth of her anger. "You can't be serious," he tells her; and to me, he says, "It's nothing. It's totally unimportant. It's all on the surface." But rather than reassuring her, his move to minimize the importance of these tiffs increases her anger. He decides to "leave her alone when she's like this. There's no point in trying to talk to her."

## Frustrating Fights

The dynamics of quarrels with fathers are often very different from the dynamics of mother/daughter quarrels. For one thing, girls know their mothers better. Once they step over the edge of early adolescence, when they are too confused by their own irritation to see things from another's perspective, girls are usually able to place a mother's outbursts in the context of the mother's needs and fears.

Meg, seventeen, reflects on how her way of fighting with her mother is shaped by her understanding of her:

> She shouts a lot, especially when she's stressed, like when she's lost and she's driving somewhere. I really hate that because it's like she's shouting at you and you feel it's your fault even though I know: No way is it my fault. I really hate it, and it's harder to take when you get older. They shouldn't—you know they shouldn't shout at you like you're a naughty kid. My dad still does it. "Hey, you!" Do they know how much that hurts? I think maybe Mom does, and at least she can be made to see what she's doing. But my dad just goes on, even in front of other people, and it gives me the most awful feeling in the pit of my stomach and then when he's finished shouting he thinks it's all over but I'm still fuming and he doesn't see what it's all about.

When Meg tries to negotiate her status vis-à-vis her father, she comes out, in her view, a loser. "It never occurs to him he can actually budge an inch on anything. You just can't get to him. He is so smug!"

Meg's father, Alan, makes a game of not budging. His enjoyment frustrates her, and he is amused by her frustration. In some ways this is positive: He endorses her opposition and her feistiness. But Meg experiences the inability to negotiate the status quo as humiliating and frustrating. Quarrels between them last for days, and Meg believes she loses status if she offers any kind of apology. She admits that she is slower to apologize to her father because he would take her apology as an admission that he was in the right and she in the wrong. Alan sees no reason why he should give way. In his view, his daughter's temper is her problem, rather than a legitimate response to him: "Meg is too quick to get hot under the collar. It's her age, I guess. And it's also her nature."

Is Meg really just a stubborn, hot-tempered teen?

Everyone likes to have some influence in a conversation. When we think of teens as being unreasonable, we aren't looking at the interaction as a whole. They may be asking for something or demanding something or objecting to something on grounds that we assess as totally unreasonable, but everyone wants to have some effect as she engages in conversation. People need to know that what they say is "taken in," that they can influence another's point of view.

If Meg apologizes to her father, he can accept the apology but "he takes it like I'm sorry I was wrong and I'm admitting he was right. Mom's more likely just to see it like: 'I'm sorry I was mean or something, not that I was wrong.'" In repairing the relationship with her father, she loses face. "So I don't say anything, and just wait a while."

Girls often said they expect a mother to feel regret about a quarrel, whoever started it, whoever's at fault. Naomi says that her mother is less likely to pull rank with her even when she's angry:

Mom can lose it more easily than my dad, but it's not a power thing. Suddenly, you know, it's all too much for her, and there's this explosion where she's shouting at everything. Then she goes out of the room and comes back like just a minute later and it's all over. My dad will still be on me next week, and he'll look at me like he's asking "Do you get my point?" We can only end the argument if I admit he's right.

Naomi is left with a dilemma. Does she end the argument and admit her father is right; or does she live "with this awful anxiety I get when he stays mad"? Unable to choose a clear route, Naomi says, "I hang about where he is and eventually he'll say something, so at least he's the first to start talking."

Girls frequently speak of a need to be "okay" with a father even when they realize they cannot persuade him to see things from their perspective. For seventeen-year-old Paula, her father is a "broadcaster" rather than a "receiver." "My dad has his ideas of things, and they're not going to change. He has a fixed mind-set of who I should be and what I should be doing. It's like—well, not like every little thing is set in his mind, but the general outline is there. So whenever something strays beyond that outline, he just shakes his head and starts broadcasting his set speech about grades and responsibilities." She has some leeway in the relationship, but not enough. She said she has "given up trying to change him. I used to get really frustrated. At thirteen I could slam my door and just writhe on the floor I was so mad at him. He's so smug. He has this: 'I'm right so I don't have to listen to you' attitude. When I come up against that I start to hate him, and then that's so awful, so I just kind of switch off and move on when I see we're about to lock horns."

A common complaint is that fathers "lecture" rather than "talk." A lecture poses as a conversation but is really a platform for the parent to speak, not listen. Mary explains: "Dad asks whether we can talk, and—it's almost funny, but it's really gross. I'm sitting down and he paces around, making these gestures with his hands, and you can tell he's enjoying the whole show. He says things like 'What you have to understand . . . ,' like he's the one who has the true perspective and he's offering it to me. So he'll be telling me what I have to understand about girls my age, or about my mom and how we could get along much better, or how I should behave, or how my life will be ruined if I get my eyebrow

pierced. And all I think is: 'How long is this going to last?'"
She has learned not to mock him openly: "Once I started to
make faces when he was mouthing off, and he goes: 'It's
time you showed respect and started listening, young lady!'
Well, you can't order someone to respect you, but there's no
point in arguing."

## Pride and Prejudice

Girls commonly complain that their fathers give them a hard
time when they speak up or fight back, but many fathers
clearly enjoy a daughter's spunk. Nevertheless, they are slow
to give way, and see no need to. A father's combination of
enjoyment and resistance can arouse fury in a daughter. Meg
sees her father as laughing at her, or finding her anger "funny."
Alan clearly is amused, but this amusement is also defensive:
Giving way costs him too much. A common male approach to
conversation as a means of confirming or upping one's status[2]
here becomes an impediment to the father/teenage daughter
relationship. Meg decides: "If I can't negotiate status, I won't
talk." Their quarrels result in greater distance. Meg, like many
teenage girls, punishes her father by giving him the cold shoulder.[3] "When he's made me really angry, I won't speak to him.
It's not necessarily the silent treatment, but I answer his questions and that's it." Eventu-ally, she gives in. "I'm still mad, but
I want to check in with him, you know, just to make sure he's
not brooding, thinking what a terrible person I am. If I think
he's okay with me, then I'll drop it. Nothing's been settled, but
I figure: Why keep on?"

If a mother sees her daughter turn away, answer curtly,
or clam up, she becomes anxious. She will pry and pester

and take abuse (usually in some variety of "Leave me alone!" or "I don't want to talk about it") in order to break through. Lack of contact is unsettling, and she is in hot pursuit of her daughter until it is reestablished. Fathers, it seems, are more likely to enjoy the peace.

## Tolerance for Conflict

If a daughter withdraws from direct conflict with a father, he will probably be more relieved than distressed. At last, he feels he is no longer under attack. Withdrawal and avoidance are reactions men understand very well.

Seeing that there can be a point and purpose to quarrels could go a long way toward helping fathers remain close and active participants in a daughter's development. Why is it more difficult for fathers than it is for mothers to learn the choreography of quarrels?

One reason is that men in general tend to be more status conscious in any conversation. Deborah Tannen outlines the different approaches men and women have to conversation in *You Just Don't Understand*: Men speak and hear a language of status and independence, whereas women speak and hear a language of connection and intimacy.[4] When preschool girls argue with other girls, they resolve conflicts rapidly through subtle shifts of compromise and evasion. Boys, on the other hand, tolerate conflict for longer, and appeal to rules and rights and threats of physical violence[5] to resolve it. While girls use a strategy of alliance and cooperation more often, and the boys use a strategy of challenge more often, both boys and girls struggle for control and are sensitive to loss of status. Both boys and girls are quick to defend themselves from humiliation or defeat, and both boys and girls try hard to get their own way. Neither girls nor boys like being wrong-footed in a conversation.

When it comes to father and daughter negotiations, fathers are more persistent at maintaining status, and quicker to frame the argument in terms of winning and losing; but the girls don't want to lose either, and don't want to compromise their position. It is the fact that daughters and fathers *share* a conversational style—and their common concern about maintaining status—that sparks the fights.

Arguments with fathers are less satisfying than are arguments with mothers, in part because men find arguments physically more stressful than do women, and therefore turn away or "stonewall" rather than remain responsive to the person they are arguing with. In a different context, psychologist John Gottman measured the heart rates of husbands and wives during quarrels.[6] He found that men's autonomic nervous system, which controls much of the body's stress response, takes, on average, longer to recover from emotional upset than does a woman's. Men are biologically more reactive to stress and become "flooded" much more quickly than women. So when men try to avoid an argument, they are probably protecting themselves from prolonged physical stress. This may be one motive for men's notorious avoidance, compared to women's impulse to "have things out" or talk it over, even when "it" is unpleasant. In a father/daughter context, a father's understanding of what his daughter is doing when she challenges or criticizes him, could reduce this flooding. If a father understood that a daughter is trying to engage him in a new way, and not rejecting him, he would see the value of staying in the battle rather than withdrawing.

Teenage daughters make few allowances for a parent who

cannot tolerate conflict. It seldom occurs to a teenage girl to keep her criticisms to herself. She delivers them with a punch because they lack dimension unless a parent in some way is shaken by them. Since she depends so much on a parent's acknowledgment of her sense of self, she demands confirmation even of her opposition to a parent.

A mother is much better at this sucker's role than a father. A father is likely to break off a blaming session before it gets rolling, whereas a mother will wait and listen, watching for some possible compromise or correction, some clue to understanding, defense, or resolution. Her greater capacity to see a daughter's point of view makes her willing to listen to these criticisms, be hurt by them, and then change in response to them.

## Just Talking: Hers and His

Mary, who, with her sister, Louise, laughs at the idea of confiding in her father, also finds her father reluctant to "just talk" or "go over things" with her the way her mother does. "He sits down with me, and if we're talking about stuff like school or a job, he listens, but most of the time you realize you're having half a conversation. I know he has opinions, like which language course to take, and which colleges to apply to, so he sort of leads the way, but only so far, and then his interest sort of dives. He's not really tuned in. I start to explain something to him, and he tells me he's sure I can figure it out for myself. If he likes what I do, he takes the credit: 'I knew you would come to that decision.' But then when he says 'Well, it's up to you,' I feel he's disapproving, but he's not going to bother to tell me. I feel—yech! horrible, squelchy inside—when he sort of disappears from the conversation and doesn't let on how he feels."

"No," her father, Trevor, remarks, after taking in her words, "I don't talk to her for hours on end like her mother does. But most of what she talks about is drivel. I try to listen to it, but it just goes around in circles. It goes on and on, and it's nothing. But that's such a small part of what we do together and who we are."

To Mary, however, it isn't "nothing" and it isn't small. Casual discussion with mothers allows girls to put out "feelers." Like a scout, they discover whether they can proceed further with revelations or questions. They investigate whether now is a good time to talk, to make a request, or lodge a complaint. Is her mother in a good mood, or is she stressed and distracted? Is she "cool" with what's going on, or do tensions from the messy bedroom, the low grade at school, the recent quarrel with a brother still lurk in the air? Listening to a daughter's "drivel" is exacting work. A mother undertakes this as she gets to know her changing daughter and her varied (sometimes clumsy, sometimes shocking, sometimes aggressive) self-presentations. Trivial, meandering conversations provide an opportunity to see what is going on in a teen's life. Things come up, which open onto something else, little details of who said what, who her current friends are, what problems she may be having, what, generally, may be troubling her.

## Mother/Daughter Talk Is Different from Woman-Talk

This mother/daughter dance does not come easily to either participant. The steps are not those of natural conversational style. Much of mother/daughter talk actually goes against the grain of woman-talk. In typical woman-talk, suggestions are put forward about what to do or how to do something. Direct instructions are avoided since, in woman-talk, issuing orders is out of conversational step. But a teenage daughter hears a mother's suggestion as worse than an order, because it seems a way of getting inside a girl's mind, asking her to think along the lines her mother thinks. In woman-talk, a common move is to share one's experience ("That happened to me." "I know just how you feel"). Normally this provides comfort through the assurance that you are understood, and not alone in your experience. But daughters do not welcome such moves from a mother. "The same things happen to me"/"I know just how you feel" threaten their efforts to prove they are very different from a mother. Daughters prefer conversations that mark areas of difference and individuality. Teens are quick to flare up, too, when mothers offer solutions to their problems, as older women often do to younger women. Teens want just the right kind of sympathy and probing: "I understand a little bit of how you feel; please tell me more"; "I want to understand, but I don't understand yet, I need you to explain it to me." To get this maternal dialogue right, mothers have to be wrong-footed many times, and have the correct steps called by their daughters.

In my studies, fathers did not see the point of such exercises. Girls preserve their relationship with a father by accepting that he will not learn this dance, and that they have to learn his terms of engagement. For example, as Naomi complains about a friend, and explains why there might be some difficulty taking her on the camping trip (because another friend will feel left out), Naomi's father, Greg, says, "We won't take her then." When Naomi comes back with "Stop telling me what to do!" Greg is puzzled and

irritable, and does not even bother to reprimand her for talking back to him or being unreasonable or ungrateful for his
help. He shrugs and carries on, and she feels he is saying
something like "Okay. Be like that."

Offering a solution to the problem the way her father does
implies, in Naomi's view, that the matter is a simple one.
Complaints about friends indicate a puzzle, which she wants
help putting together. Shutting her friend out isn't the
answer; it leads to more problems. Besides, how do you go
about saying to a friend you don't want her to come? Her
mother helps her by suggesting a context to explain this.
"You could tell her we thought it was okay, but now we think
it should just be a family trip, and your brother isn't taking
anyone either, and maybe we'll do something with her
another time." Of course, Naomi initially reject this suggestion ("I can't say that. That's stupid.") but gradually she modifies it so she can use it. She needs to think about how disappointed her friend will be, and of course whether this will
make the uneasy relationship worse. When she begins to
talk about this her father sees her as vacillating, irrational.
There is no point in advising her, he concludes, because she
cannot make up her mind. What she wants, however, is an
extended conversation that will help her map out the problem and make up her mind.

## Daddy's Girl

There is no doubt that fathers play an important role in a
girl's life, and that this importance has an abiding effect on
her personal happiness. Most girls say they love their
fathers; some say they admire him "more than any other
man." When they think of closeness in terms of talking,

relaxing, doing their own thing, they say they are "not really close." Nevertheless, they also tend to speak warmly about the activities they share with a father, even if they are activities that involve his preferences and not theirs, such as hiking, studying, or baseball.

When adult women reflect on the role a father played in their development, they often credit his encouragement with their success. In midlife, women often try to link up anew with a father. They catch sight of a vulnerable side they did not always see when they were younger.[7] In retrospect, women say their fathers did play an important part in their development during adolescence.

As in all close relationships, there are two different stories to any father/daughter love. Fathers believe that they know their daughters better as teens than they knew them in childhood. They themselves feel more competent and comfortable with them, better able to engage them in a range of activities and on different levels. Greg is pleased by Naomi's increased stamina, which allows him to take her on rigorous hikes. "When she was little she'd get tired, and she was such a pain in the neck. Now I have trouble keeping up with her. I can do more with her. Yeah, we're closer now."

But girls have a different view. They feel less close to their fathers as teens than as kids. They feel that their fathers are now in some ways less comfortable with them. They describe them as less indulgent and less gentle. But women, looking back on their teen years, see a father as a strong influence and cite his encouragement as a source of lifelong confidence.

The looking-back accounts of a father's importance are supported by recent research on the long-term impact of a father's involvement with his teenage daughter, which shows particularly strong association between fathers' involvement with daughters during adolescence and good psychological health in later life.[8] While teens themselves, quick to complain about any adult, frequently think a father is insufficiently interested in the minutiae of their lives, his involvement is correlated with greater success, both personal and professional, in adulthood.

Involvement means taking an interest in her education— assessing it, talking her through the options and decisions— seeking her companionship, teaching her things. Whether he is looking through a college prospectus with her or going grocery shopping with her, he engages her in a crucial parent/child relationship.

Involvement does not necessarily mean living in the same house as a daughter, though the teenage girls in my study were devastated when a father did leave home. Old enough in some sense to understand and provide sympathy and tolerate the financial changes often associated with parents' divorce, teenage girls nonetheless spoke of the profound disappointment they felt. When Naomi's father left her mother, she said that coming home from school "is awful now, because I know he won't be coming home later. He sometimes comes by, but it's not the same." A year later, she has to deal with the fact that other teenage girls, now her stepsisters, are living in his house. "I know this makes me sound like a spoiled brat, but I can't stand the thought of him living with them, and them having him, and his doing stuff with them. Sometimes I think I just can't bear it. And then he'll say something, and I realize that whatever else happens in his life, I'll still be his daughter the way I used to be. When that happens, I feel glorious. Suddenly that awful feeling's gone."

Senka, whose parents divorced when she was fourteen, is anxious about losing contact with her father. She is obsessive about dividing her time between her mother and father. She counts each hour, and "makes up" time the following week, if she spends more time with her mother. Most teenage girls are proactive in maintaining contact with a father.[9] They put up with doing what he wants to do in order to be with him.

## When a Father Mothers

One fascinating question is whether a father/daughter relationship is different if the father is the custodial parent, the one who deals out care and control single-handedly on a daily basis.

In my study I found there was a difference—but not a structural one. The relationship itself—with the tiffs framed by a father's hierarchical form of argument, with shared interests bounded by his own interests, with refusal to dance through an argument—is remarkably similar in custodial fathers to that of other involved fathers.

Emma, seventeen, and Elizabeth, eighteen, have lived with their father since their parents' divorce four years ago. They speak about their father very much in the terms used by Mary, Louise, and Naomi. In some respects, the common father/teenage daughter problems are compounded by the special relationship they have with a single father who raises them.

Careful, as most teenagers are, to keep contact with a nonresident parent, they go to their mother, definitely not their father ("Talk to Dad about this stuff? No way!") with questions about gynecological health, sex, and boyfriends. In their case, too, in spite of the divorce, their mother acts as mediator between the girls and their father. Their mother, Elsa, helps them deal with their father's impatience by telling them "not to take it personally." She explains, "He really does give you the benefit of the doubt—though that's not always obvious from his first response!"

The sisters were thirteen and fourteen when their parents separated. Their maturity and independence, they said, made it easier to choose to stay with their father. He stayed in their hometown, while their mother moved away. They also felt she was "delicate and maybe needed her own space for a while." They were beyond the "tucking-in stage." Nevertheless, they appreciate his caretaking gestures, such as keeping their dinner warm if they are out late, coming home to lunch if they are ill, and teaching them to maintain and repair their bicycles.

As Emma and Elizabeth speak about their father, they separate out various time spans—what they felt about him when he and their mother first separated, how they were for a while after that, and how things changed when their father remarried.

Initially they had blamed their mother for "leaving, just going away," but now they realize how much that blame hurt her. They want to repair that harm by understanding her, and they realize, too, that they are still very close to her. She addresses their continuing but usually controlled needs to be "mothered." They describe a recent event that brought this into focus. Emma was coming home from orchestra practice at about 9:30 in the evening:

> When I got to the door I could see someone moving inside. I knew it wasn't my sister, and I thought maybe Dad had come back early [from an out-of-town conference], but then I knew it wasn't Dad either, because I could see him run out the back when I put my key in the door. I froze. I just didn't know what to do, so I phoned my dad's cell and he was cool

as ice. He just told me what to do and not go inside until the police came, and that was it. He didn't ask how I felt or anything. I rang Mom and she was really good, really involved. She told me not to worry because the intruder wouldn't come back and was only after easy stuff, but she then arranged for me to spend the night at a friend of hers and she came down the next day. It was like she knew just how spooked I was, not like my dad who wanted to know was I okay and that was the end of it.

A current problem Emma has with her father also revolves around his failure to understand how she feels—in particular, how she feels about the current plans to sell the house. Quarrels spark as she tries to explain her regret at moving. He, in turn, imputes motives to her; while she accuses him of not listening.

We moved here only two years ago, after we sold the house that I'd grown up in. Now my Dad and stepmother are going to sell this one, because my stepmother wants some fancy house farther out of town. When I started to tell him how sad that made me, he slammed his hand on the table and said, "We've been through all this before!" Like he's decided and he's had his say and that's that. Then he blew up at me because he was showing someone around the house and my bedroom was a mess. He told me I'd done it on purpose because I didn't want to move. That really made me sick. I mean, anyone can forget to clean up a room! But he was sort of saying, "You're sneaky and I can't trust you." He wouldn't listen when I tried to tell him it wasn't on purpose.

Now Emma is planning to go to college, and she comes up against what she sees as the limits of his love. As her father and stepmother prepare to move to a different house, she feels she is being edged out of her real home. "He says we can always come to stay, and doesn't understand why I feel so low about it. He talks about having done his duty by us and we're old enough to be independent. He says if we want to be like kids in a parent's home, our mother can take her turn now. When he says that, I feel I should move in with Mom tomorrow and never speak to him again."

The reference to "duty" separates his care, which she had once so appreciated, from love. "I know I'll always be one of the most important things in my mother's life. I know I'll always have a home with her. My father loves me even less than I thought he did."

Yet teenage girls switch with alarming ease from assessments of a parent's love as "useless" to an overwhelming appreciation of its value. One week later, Emma says, "He does want us around—but more or less on his terms. We can't talk to him the way we used to. It's all changed [since he remarried]. He doesn't seem to have much time for us. He used to tell us what he was doing, how his research was going, that sort of thing. I used to tell him lots of things that happened in school, or whatever. We used to laugh about it. At first I thought he'd notice I was keeping something back, and try to persuade me to talk. But he doesn't even notice. I could disappear inside and he wouldn't notice."

While mothers do notice when a daughter "clams up" or "isn't talking," and take withdrawal as a worrying sign, and nag and cajole a silent daughter into speech, fathers are more likely to "let her keep quiet if she wants to," and "are glad for a bit of peace and quiet."

Yet, watching these girls with their father, there is clearly a powerful bond. His jokes are not especially funny to an outsider. He concocts doggerel rhymes and invites his daughters to invent the next line. He makes coded remarks using initials in place of words, and instigates guessing games about their meaning. The three are fully engaged in these games.

When I ask Emma whether her stepmother ever participates in such verbal play, she says, "Oh, no, that's always been just me, my sister, and my dad."

Emma and Elizabeth may have felt the limits of a father's love, but they are noting the boundaries of a substantial bond.

## *Father/Daughter Facts:*

- Teenage girls value their connection to a father.
- Fathers are eager to extend their involvement with their daughters when they mature and are able to engage with them in new ways.
- Girls eagerly accept these "extension offers" but also develop defenses against the limitations of closeness to a father.
- This defense involves withdrawal, curtailment of personal information, and silence. As a result, girls sometimes describe themselves as "not close" to a father. Fathers are outraged by this description because they see more clearly than their daughters do at present how close they are.
- Mothers often mediate between father and daughter by acknowledging the daughter's anger while trying to minimize the insult or hurtful intentions of the father.
- Many women, looking back on their teen years, say that they were close to their fathers.

## What Can a Father Do?

Teens want to have a close relationship with their fathers. They withdraw when they feel insulted or hurt, but they do not stay away for long. It does not take much for a father to improve his connection to a daughter.

- Try to notice when you are listening, versus when you are lecturing. Are you thinking only of what you want to say? Are you interrupting her/shouting her down/telling her she doesn't listen?
- Talk around a problem; avoid offering a solution or giving simple advice. You want to help her, but she won't be convinced of your advice unless she is confident that you understand the problem. Ask a few questions about it. Even when the points seem minor, they are important to her.
- Take her anger seriously: Respect it; don't ridicule it. This means no laughing at her tears or shouting. It will also be effective to ask why she is angry, rather than declaring her anger "unreasonable."
- If she doesn't talk, don't be thankful for the peace and quiet; engage her. If you need a break from an argument, then take it, but return to the discussion when you have calmed down.
- Continue to involve her in your interests, but try to explore hers, too.
- Remember that she is not as confident in opposition to you as she appears. There is no need to insist that you are right and she is wrong; she half believes that already.

# 9.

# *"I'm too fat!"*: *The Ambiguity of Physical Growth*

## Changing Problems

Three decades ago, mothers worried more about a teenage girl eating too much and getting fat than they did about her obsession with being thin. An overweight girl was likely to be teased, unlikely to be chosen as a friend. "Being fat" was thought to be a self-inflicted and self-reinforcing condition brought on by self-indulgence and low self-esteem; being "too fat" would lead to being "even fatter" as self-pity and iso-lation provided conditions for comfort eating. When I first began research on mothers and daughters in the mid-1980s, girls frequently complained that their mothers constantly warned them against "eating too much" and "getting fat."

Today, mothers are far more likely to worry that a daugh-ter is refusing to eat well and to eat enough. Early dieting—before age fifteen—was particularly upsetting. To counter the social currents driving girls toward dissatisfaction, the mothers in my most recent study took pains to admire a daughter's appearance. They want their daughters to feel good about the bodies they have, and they want to help them resist the cult of thinness. They are intent on correcting their own mothers' warning about gaining weight. They avoid comments, too, about the dangers of "showing your breasts" or "putting yourself on display" as they follow up their positive messages to a daughter that she should be comfortable with the body she has. "I tell her she is just fine, just as she is," Vicky says, but she also feels powerless against the barrage of skinny ideals.

"I feel like I'm batting away some crazy image in her mind. I get it under control, and then she goes out and sucks up more of that junk. She pores over *Glamour* magazine, and then she goes to the hall mirror, and then she goes to the bathroom mirror, and then she stands on a chair to look in the mirror in her bedroom. She says she's fat, and I say, 'Where's the fat?' and she says, 'You can't see my ribs,' and that's her notion of not being fat," Alex's mother, Vicky, says. "She spends half an hour at a time in the bathroom. I can hear her stepping on the scales over and over again. I say she looks just fine, but what I say cuts no ice. Right?" Vicky asks, turning to Alex, who stares her mother's smile away and replies brusquely, "You're more fixated on your weight than I am."

The accusation stops Vicky cold. "It's not true," she insists. "I'm not as bad as she is. But it's still an issue with me, even when I want to know better." In this context of uncertainty, quarrels were likely to upset both mother and daughter. In fact, on this topic, quarrels were seldom direct and open.

One reason women are so puzzled about how to help girls establish a positive body image is that they, too, are influenced by the ideals they want their daughters to discount. As we worry about our daughters' obsession with weight and appearance, for example, we might notice that as women we carry on this social preoccupation. While mothers try to persuade their daughters to eat enough and to eat well, they themselves may be dieters and worry about "looking fat." They swear at a favorite suit for suddenly being "too small." They express concern about weight among their friends. Just observe women greeting each other: "You look terrific," says one. "Did you lose weight?" And the other laughs, unwilling to accept the compliment: "I wish!" The greeting ritual continues with mutual discussion of looks and weight before other topics are broached—news of job and family and other friends that paint pictures of success or failure.[1]

Many girls are daughters of dieters. Family meals easily become a forum for what Mimi Nichter[2] calls "fat talk": "I shouldn't eat this." "I've already eaten so much today." "I want to be able to fit into that suit by the end of the month," women say, and their daughters hear them. And, in spite of their fear that a daughter will be gripped by the anorexic-fostering culture, mothers feel responsible for a daughter's appearance, and monitor her caloric intake ("Why don't you be good and skip dessert tonight"). Fathers, too, join the weight police by remarking on a daughter's size or appetite. Given a teenage girl's hypersensitivity to her appearance, a remark that might be intended as gentle teasing can crush her.

Mothers are not the cause of their daughter's bad body image; but women do sometimes bring that much closer to a daughter the very culture they would like to change. Becky's mother, Sharon, says, "I'm at my wits' end. Ever since she turned thirteen, she's been talking about her so-called fat stomach and fat thighs. She even complains about her fat nose." Sharon would like to take on the glamour culture that breeds dissatisfaction in her daughter, but she is also anxious about her own complicity. "I guess I worry, too, about looking fat, and heaven knows, I go on a diet, and then break my diet. But Becky's gorgeous, and I tell her she's gorgeous, but it just doesn't go in." Sharon hopes she can provide Becky with a sane assessment of her appearance, but Becky is unlikely to steer clear of these pressures when she sees that her mother is in the grip of mainstream ideals.

Of course, girls experience their physical self through a father, too. Jennifer notes her father, Dale's, unease at her physical development. She feels she has lost the child's body that allowed her to have a simple and unselfconscious relationship with her dad. She ridicules her father for pretending "not to notice anything, like even when I'm in a swimsuit, he looks everywhere else but at my chest." Does growing up have to mean that she loses this precious relationship? she wonders. When her father asks, "Are you going to eat all of that?" or "That's not what you should eat if you want to lose weight" or "You keep eating like that and you'll get fat," she feels "like he's kicked me, and he just hates how I look."

Friends also force the message home. Teenagers begin to diet when their friends do. They are quick to notice who has gained or lost a few pounds. They shop together, and hang out in changing rooms to assess clothes, to discuss their image in these clothes ("Wow, you look really cool," or "You're a real fashion chick"), to construct a lifestyle around the clothes ("You'll have a great time clubbing when you wear that," and "You should wear that after the football game" or "That's what you should wear to make an impression at that party"), and to ask one another, as they look in a full-length mirror, "Do I look fat in this?" Adolescent boys are not the ones watching in this way. In fact, girls are far more critical of one another than boys are. Boys don't read *Glamour* or *Seventeen* and scrutinize the models to judge who has the "perfect" face, the "nicest hair," or who "isn't really pretty." Girls do—and they do it together.

Walking in the mall with her friends, Becky's attention is drawn by her friend Jennifer to a slender, long-legged girl browsing in a boutique. "Don't you wish you looked like her?" Jennifer asks. Becky tells me later, "When Jen asked me that, it's like she punched me in the stomach. I think: Here my friend is admiring someone else. What good am I? Why does she bother to hang out with me? She doesn't think I'm good to look at, and she doesn't feel good about herself when she's with me. I might as well not be there."

On good days, she and Jennifer do make each other feel good. In the mall boutiques they focus on each other, trying on clothes, admiring and enjoying each other. They are excited by a new top or a new pair of jeans, and talk about where they would wear this or that, whether something is "cool," who else in their world (either someone at school or a well-known actress) has a top like this one. On these days, each is acceptable to the other without the rider "If only I/you could lose fifteen pounds." They are fine as they are. Life can be sweet, just as they are. But on some days, they look in the mirror, or down at their thighs, and say, repeatedly, almost compulsively, "I'm so fat." Sharon says, "Someone only has to look at Becky for her to cringe and say, 'I'm never going to wear these jeans again. I look so fat.'"

For a teen, there is no such thing as neutral observation. When people see you, they are either admiring or critical, and either response is confusing. The confusion cuts deep into our social culture. While, on the one hand, girls, as kids, are responding to pressure to appear sexual and savvy at a very early age, they are also under pressure to maintain a prepubescent figure. At age ten and eleven, girls are labeled "tweens" rather than kids because, while not yet teenagers, they appear far more teen than kid. Their clothes are meticulously chosen, each detail in keeping with a fashion statement easily interpreted by their peers. They apply a vast array of makeup, from eyeliner to body glitter, with well-practiced ease. Their eyebrows are plucked and their eyelashes are curled. They aim to look cool, wise, and confident.

Forward-looking though they are in street style and street wisdom, they look backward as they set their physical ideal. The body they wish to have is pubescent rather than adolescent. Long legs, thin thighs, small or "neat" breasts, as many girls described their ideal body, belong to the proportions of today's eleven- or twelve-year-old, which is now the average age for the onset of menstruation.

Teenage girls seem to have lost the ability to gauge what normal is for a woman's physique. I handed a group of ten thirteen-year-olds a pile of photographs showing girls of varying ages. I asked them to sort them into age groups. The minds of these bright and observant girls seemed to seize up. While some thought a well-developed eighteen-year-old was merely thirteen, the most common confusion was to classify photographs of thirteen-year-olds in the sixteen- to seventeen-year-old range. In other words, they thought a normal sixteen- or seventeen-year-old should look the way a normal thirteen-year-old actually does look. How could they judge whether they themselves were "too big" or "fat" if they fell prey to the notion that a sixteen-year-old should look like someone just at the start of puberty?

These girls are up against pressure from a beauty culture

that is constantly criticized and constantly reinforced. While politicians and parents clamor for a wider range of models, the fashion and food industries present ever more stringent physiques. The average weight of female fashion models is now ten pounds lower than it was thirty years ago. Teenage girls are more focused than ever before, and from an earlier age, on models and actresses whose profession is to set iconic standards of shape and size. As Vicky says, "I get mad at those magazines she loves, and then I start shouting at her, and she just shrugs. I can hear her thinking: 'That woman is nuts.' I just wish she wasn't so involved in her looks, and I tell her that and she just lets out this big sigh. She says she could forget about her looks if she wasn't fat."

The so-called self-involvement of adolescents, the new focus on "looks"—on clothes, on the looks-altering decorations ranging from makeup to body piercing—are ways of dealing with self-consciousness. Fat becomes a word to cover anything that isn't the familiar child body.

## Growth Spurts

Teenage girls are just beginning, consciously, to look at their mothers and think, "Will I develop in that way? Is my future body going to be like that body?" And as they see their bodies mature into women's bodies, they also feel the pressure of an earlier unconscious identification with a mother. In effect, they feel they are becoming a different person. Their intensive grooming, when their bodies become a project to work on,[3] is a way of gaining familiarity with this new self and, hopefully, gaining some control over it.

In Carson McCullers's novel *The Member of the Wedding*, twelve-year-old Frankie looks in the mirror and considers what she will one day become. Having grown four inches in the past year, she calculates that, at this rate, she will be nine feet tall by the time she can count on being fully grown. Unless she can stop herself, she will shortly become a freak.

Frankie's fear of her future body is both logical (we see her plotting the growth graph) and ridiculous. "Growth spurts" are particularly fast rates of growth, but they are inevitably brief. When girls fill out over a short time span, they may feel they are being carried forward by an unstoppable and unwelcome force. At the cusp of adolescence, growing up takes on a new and often ambivalent meaning. A child is eager to be older, taller, more grown-up. "My, haven't you grown!" a familiar adult response to meeting a child, registers a child's own pride in her pace of development. Becky notes that when family friends and relatives visit, they no longer speak with the same easy pride as they take note of her growth. Their looks, Becky explains, "are sort of embarrassed, really. You can see them trying not to look, and trying not to show what they really mean when they say I'm such a big girl now. I never know whether they're thinking Gosh! in a good way, which is what they pretend to think, or 'fat' or 'ruined,' which are the words I'm always afraid are really in their minds."

Sharon says, "That's ridiculous. They're thinking how stunning you are." Becky says, "I don't know what they're thinking. You don't know what they're thinking. They're not going to tell you, are they? But it feels like they're embarrassed, and it's horrible. They embarrass me. I never want to see them again. I hate them!"

So mother and daughter embark on a quarrel about gratitude and fairness of mind to old family friends, while Becky is nursing the wounds of an encounter that she experiences as an attack. She describes her sense that, when people look at her, their eyes "scrape my skin raw"; being in a roomful of people is like "being hedged in by barbed wire, and every movement hurts."

Her growth represents sexual maturity, and both mother and daughter may be ambivalent about this. Each is excited and fascinated by a girl's maturity, but sometimes the changes seem "too fast" or "drastic." While some girls are keen observers of bodily changes, and feel actively involved in their development ("Look what's happening to me!" "I have to keep up with this." "I now should lay claim to my greater maturity"), Becky, in midadolescence, speaks about a disrupted self.

Becky gets out clothes she wore last summer and wonders how they could have belonged to her. She reflects on what growing was like when she was a kid, how she would suddenly realize she could reach the shelf that was once too high for her. Now she feels that her body "is running away from itself." She feels "too big" to cuddle her mother. She feels she does not "fit." She describes her "surprise, which was like a slap of shame" when she realized she could no longer sit in her childhood rocker. "Before, growing meant I could do more things. Now it means there are things I can't do. Two years ago I had the perfect body for gymnastics. That was me, that was who I was—this girl who was a wow at gymnastics. Now I'm fourteen, and it isn't me. I can still do the moves, but that isn't enough. And now performing is torture. I can't stand people watching me anymore. And a year ago I didn't think about it. So now—"

Becky bites her lips, frowns, and turns away. She is angry

because she is crying, and I might offer sympathy, and that might increase her vulnerability. She wants to prove she doesn't care, that giving up gymnastics was her idea.

She describes her mother as "nagging her about stuff" and about gym in particular. "She has this bee in her bonnet about sports, like it's the thing that's going to save me from dropping out and committing suicide or something. She says I'm putting on weight because I don't get enough exercise, and she doesn't see that I don't get enough exercise because I've put on weight. My body just isn't me anymore, and I hate it."

So we hear from Becky that her mother does talk to her about weight gain as a problem. Sharon couches her concern in terms of health and exercise, but Becky hears the subtext: You are in danger of getting too fat. When Sharon confronts this, she is, understandably, heated in her own defense: "I can't sit back and watch her put on those lazy pounds without saying anything." And Becky says, "But you say stuff and then you don't say it. You say I look great just as I am and then you warn me about eating too much." Mother and daughter glare at each other, at a stalemate, caught in the web of cultural confusions. Becky tells me later, "She can make me so mad I want to spit, but we don't argue about weight. What am I supposed to say? 'I don't care if I'm fat?' No, I just give her a look, and then she either shuts up or starts complaining about my attitude, and then we argue about that."

## Real Eating Troubles

Eating disorders are rare—only 10 percent of girls in Western culture (and fewer in other cultures) are affected by them.

What is so disturbing to mothers, however, is that these rare conditions are clearly linked to ordinary day-to-day experiences. Anorexia has become a specter for mothers as their teens express concern about eating too much, berate themselves for being "piggish" or "disgusting," assesses their size and shape in the mirror, and weigh themselves several times a day.

Anorexia is an illness with the highest mortality rate of any psychiatric illness and is notoriously difficult to treat. In a long-term follow-up of women with anorexia, 7 percent of anorexia sufferers had died after ten years.[4] Although anorexia is now thought to have a genetic link, it is triggered by a desire to lose weight. The dieting then becomes compulsive. Gripped by the "success" of dieting, an anorexic's self-perception is so distorted that all body fat, even that necessary to healthy function, seems like "fat," in the sense of "too fat." Brain scans on anorexic girls show disturbances in the part of the brain dealing with appetite and visual perception[5]; but these recent findings simply confirm what was already known: The anorexic's perceptions become so warped that, however thin she becomes, she sees herself in danger of becoming too fat. And this distorted view is endorsed in a wide cultural context: The ideal physique, as portrayed by models, mannequins, and many actresses, is that of a person in a state of starvation.

Food becomes a source of anxiety and terror because it represents the prospect of weight gain. If she is "bad" and eats, she exercises to work off any calories she has consumed either through social pressure or lack of willpower. "Eating makes me feel awful," Phoebe, sixteen, explains. "Just the thought that I'm going to eat makes me anxious, and then if I do eat, I'm worried I won't stop in time, like I'll eat too much? And then I have to worry about whether I should try—you know—try to get rid of it, and then I have to think about how and when. And I also feel—I just feel guilty. It's a lot easier just being hungry. When I'm really hungry, with that white kind of tension evenly distributed in every part of my stomach, I feel really good. I feel proud."

Phoebe began her rigorous diet two years ago. "When I was thirteen, I was really fat." Weight loss only started being obviously problematic six months ago when she discovered she was twenty pounds below her original target weight, but she refused to "break faith with my diet." She is ambivalent about her condition. "It's hard to stop. I still get this sense of achievement when the scales are lower today than they were yesterday. I tell my mom that I want to put on weight, and in some sense I do, but I also think how lucky I am to be on this side of the fence. The worst thing would be to find I was suddenly fat again."

While Phoebe's mother, Thea, sees her daughter as "out of control," Phoebe sees herself as a good self-manager. She avoids many of the problems normal girls face. She does not have to deal with growth spurts. Self-induced starvation puts a halt to that. She does not have to deal with the most obvious signal of fertility. Malnutrition puts a stop to her periods. She won't be embarrassed by others' tendency to look (whether admiringly or critically) at her breasts, since she has no curves made up of body fat. Starvation cancels the mature woman in her. A sixteen-year-old anorexic girl can regain a little girl's physique and destroy a mature girl's body rhythms. For Phoebe, this seems like an achievement.

"We don't even argue about this," Thea says, "because she's so cool about it. I tell her she's about to drop dead, and she tells me she's fine. I tell her she looks terrible, and she laughs. There is just no engagement here."

While Phoebe, suffering from anorexia, seems frail, and is in fact in physical danger, she describes herself as strong. She feels strong because she has the strength to overcome her appetites. She also feels strong in the sense of being independent: She does not need food—see how she survives without it. She sees herself as supremely self-sufficient.

Thea describes the terror of mealtimes. "Phoebe's illness affects the whole family. We insist that she sit with us, but then for a long time we let her pretend to eat, and we thought that if we only didn't pay attention, she'd relax and be okay. But we couldn't relax. It was torture for us all. Her little sister is heartbroken over this, and sometimes feels bad for being able to eat. I tried giving her tiny portions, sort of saying, Well, at least try this; I'm not asking much of you. But now I say: I'm not going to let you starve. I'm not letting you out of my sight until you do this. At first, she didn't pay any attention, but now she's starting to get rattled. She says, 'You can't *make* me eat,' and I tell her that's just what I'll do if I have to."

Thea has learned to be ferociously protective of Phoebe, and to withstand all quarrels in order to save her.[6] She takes the line that cannot work as a general rule, but which sometimes has to be followed: "I'm not going to negotiate this one!" Nell and her daughter Liz deal with a similar problem, but one where it is more difficult for the mother to be sure of her position. Bulimia is an eating disorder with different symptoms from anorexia, but has related psychology. It is less visible because body weight is maintained. Bulimia involves intense preoccupation with body weight and shape, with regular episodes of uncontrolled overeating, followed by extreme methods (vomiting and laxative use) to counter-act the feared effects of overeating. It is less public than anorexia, because bulimic girls tend to maintain their weight (while eating vast amounts) rather than lose weight. They may appear to eat normally in front of others and binge when alone. Like anorexia, it is a disorder with the staying power of an addiction.

Liz says she has been bulimic for two years. At seventeen, she is a normal weight, but, like many other seventeen-year-old girls, fights fat that "wants to find its way into me." She offers to do the family shopping on the way home from school, and then does parallel shopping for herself. This is easier since she has been able to drive, because she can carry more, and because she can hide her food in the car if anyone is in the kitchen when she unloads. The condition drives her lifestyle. Eating and finding ways to purge are constantly in her thoughts.

She views her condition as a clever strategy for weight control. "I know what it seems like to you. I know what how everyone else would see it, but it really doesn't bother me. This way I can eat and I don't have to get fat." For her, this is a way of beating the system.

But when we talk about when she is likely to eat, and how she feels, she registers her problems. She would like to be able to eat without then being gripped by a compulsion to overeat. While bingeing, she feels she is gripped by a frenzy. "That's what's disgusting—not the purging, but the devour-ing." She binges when she is anxious, and yes, she admits, she is generally deeply unhappy. She does not see how anyone in her family would help. "I do what I can to keep it away from them, but I don't do it all that well. They're blind not to know what I'm doing. But it wouldn't help if they did know. They'd just fuss and yell, and I'd just have to be more careful. I wouldn't stop."

Nell is not "blind," and she does worry that "Liz sometimes does things to get rid of what she eats," but she has no idea of the extent of Liz's habit. "Liz needs her privacy. She likes being alone a lot. She hates being interrupted. I can sympathize with that." So the mother's delicacy actually accommodates her daughter's destructive habit. Nell and Liz will have to uncover their fears and secrets in a quarrel before they can open up to each other.

## Countering the Cult of Thinness

Mothers may sometimes set bad examples, as they stand side by side with their daughters, amid the cultural ideal of thinness. But neither we nor our daughters are rendered helpless by these ideals.[7] Like Vicky and Sharon, many mothers of teenage girls try to protect their daughters from pressures to be thin and from their own proneness to being critical of their looks. Taking on board the influence of ads, models, films, and fashion, they say they want "to make her pleased with the changes in her body" and to "make her happy with how she looks."

Alex and Becky, like many daughters, discount a mother's view. "She thinks I'm pretty because I'm her daughter." "She doesn't know anything." "She has to say I'm pretty." But if we assess ourselves for consistency, our daughters will find it more difficult to dismiss our contentment with their bodies, just as they are. As we have seen, it is the mixed messages from a mother that distance Alex and Becky from maternal reassurance.

- Though mothers are often themselves caught in the I-wish-I-were-thinner net, they can work with their daughters to learn from those girls who shake themselves free.[8] Vicky, who despairs at the envy her daughter suffers over another girl's long, thin legs, could join her daughter in establishing a range of different descriptions of bodies. She and her daughter could work together to shift from thoughts such as "I wish I had legs like that" or "See, no one has a nose like mine" to describing women's legs in terms of punch and power. "They look really strong" or "She looks firm and steady." The point is to change the vocabulary from "gorgeous" to "go-getting."
- Sharon could accept Becky's accusations that she gives mixed messages. In fact, many mothers could come right out and admit: "I am confused, too, about how important it is to be thin." Teenage girls are eager to reflect on the problems they experience in a confused state. When a mother talks about her own confusion, and perhaps explains how the pressures to be thin stay with her, even while she has learned to resist the obsession and envy that tend to plague teenage girls, then a daughter herself feels less ashamed, and less powerless in her envy of other girls' physiques. Mother and daughter together can ease the pressures from the ideal.
- Mothers can call others to account: When family friends and relatives exclaim with double meaning, "How you've grown," Sharon could say, "Yes, she's really developed over the past year. In all sorts of ways," and stare down

their embarrassment. In this way she is signaling that she knows what they are talking about, and that her daughter does, too; and she is also forming an alliance with Becky, fielding the embarrassment, taking it on herself.

If our daughter is not eating enough, then we can send an "I'm not going to let you hurt yourself" message. This is difficult, and may escalate conflict—but there is no choice. Most mothers are worried about nagging a daughter about food—whether it's about eating too much or eating too little. We are punished by our daughters for "nagging" because they are so sensitive to it. Sometimes we can use this power to indicate that they are simply not going to get away with harming themselves.

- We can keep repeating the message that girls seem to discount: that she looks good as she is, that all bodies are different, that her own is special and valuable. It will become a mental reference, which eventually will challenge her self-dissatisfaction.
- It appears that one way of guarding against some more extreme eating disorders is to encourage assertiveness. So mothers can encourage a daughter by allowing her to "talk back" and "speak up." After all, what is often called "lip" isn't all bad. Teenagers express their feelings in strong language. We can encourage their "attitude," even if that attitude opposes us. We can help them swagger.
- We can focus on other things, in particular, on what her body can do, what she wants it to do, how it works as a source of feeling and strength. Mother and daughter together can move away from "fat talk."

# 10.    *"I know that already!":*
*Sex Talk*

## The Modern Mom

"The last thing I want is for her to feel there are things she just can't say to me. Being open—her with me, me with her, is just about the most important thing in our relationship."

Mothers act as guardians and disciplinarians and guides, and in the midst of their intense life with a teenage daughter, they seek frank and open discussions about the sexuality they sometimes fear and which a daughter feels powerfully but may not understand. Lisette speaks of her hope for mutual discussion, in stark contrast to the conversations she was able to conduct with her own mother. She grew up in a household in which any mention of sexual activity was for adults only, "But at the same time we were pretty much dependent on the grown-ups for telling us all about it. My mother told me the bare facts, sort of all in one go. She delivered this prepared speech and seemed relieved when she finished. At school we had one session where the girls were sent into a room and a woman we'd never seen before told us about sanitary towels and our changing bodies. I learned most from my older sister, and I heard really weird stuff from my friends, whose mothers were more uptight than mine, but then I was eighteen, and suddenly everyone knew everything and everyone was talking about sex, and my parents' attitude seemed so outdated and so unnecessary."

Reflecting on her own adolescence, Lisette said she felt "cheated, and really disappointed when my mom gave me the bare facts, and indicated that was the end of her speech. I wanted to mull it over and ask questions. I wanted to get some understanding of how it all fit into that controlled adult framework. But I got nothing more. I'll tell Anna anything she wants."

## Encouraging Sensual Awareness

At one time, a common worry was that openness about sex would encourage early sexual activity by instilling young people with lustful thoughts. Now it is widely recognized that what is called sex education is essential to lowering the risk of teenage pregnancy and sexually transmitted diseases. But just as important as facts about health and fertility are facts about emotions and pleasures linked to sex.

Teenage girls who describe mothers as open and easy to talk to are likely to associate sex with their own pleasure. They describe the sensuality of childhood play—running around naked in the backyard, or skinny-dipping in streams, feeling a cat's fur on their bare chests when they get out of a bath, being tickled and thrilled by a dog's tongue on their feet. They often acknowledge masturbation, which they see as self-exploration rather than defilement. They have been encouraged to search for the body's sensual wellsprings and have far more control over their early sexual experiences.

The girls who speak about a wide range of sensual experiences are likely to know, beforehand, when they are about to have their first sexual experience.[1]

The myth that young girls are impelled into sexual activity by the power of desire still holds fast; and therefore, it is thought that the most important messages to give are about constraint and control: Sex exposes one to the complications of pregnancy and the dangers of disease. While we accept that teens work at being attractive and sexy, we advise them to say "no."

In fact, one of the most powerful and protective messages a mother can give to her daughter is: "Your pleasure and desire are significant; learn to identify and value your own responses." Girls who are aware of their own desire and see it as a central factor in their decisions about sexual activity are more likely to acknowledge what they are doing. They are less likely to get pregnant because they are more likely to know what they are about to do, plan ahead, and therefore to use birth control.[2]

In contrast, some girls who do not speak to a mother about the emotional and pleasurable aspects of sex say of their first sexual experience that they didn't know what was happening, they didn't know it could happen so quickly, they didn't know it could happen just like that. They see sexual activity as initiated by a partner's desires, and so it happens on someone else's terms.

It is conversation about pleasure, as much as care, that is crucial to a girl's sexual education, even in a society in which this education is offered within schools and is prominent in the media: Being able to place her own feelings in the forefront of her mind is protection against passivity and ignorance.

## Sexual Entitlement

Sexual desire can become a source of personal knowledge and personal power. Teenagers try to read the mysterious meanings of others' responses to them and of their own desires, many of which are just beyond their comprehension. They try to gauge their needs and the nature of their attachments. They worry, in very different ways, about issues of sexual closeness and personal boundaries. Sonia, eighteen, asks: "If I sometimes feel sexually repelled by a man, does it mean I don't like him?" and "How attracted do I have to be to someone to want to sleep with him?" Fran, seventeen, wonders: "How can I love someone and want a continuing relationship with him, but so easily have enough of him sexually and so often find solitude so pleasurable?" Lara, nineteen, asks: "If someone doesn't want to make love with me, does that mean he doesn't love me? Do I want sex too much?" Other young people face even more complex questions. Nisha, at sixteen, reframes her sexuality as she identifies herself as a lesbian. While on the one hand she is exhilarated by naming the feelings she has experienced as both immutable and unthinkable, she now faces a host of new questions: "Does my new recognition of my sexuality change my identity?" and "How does it affect my friendships?" and, of course, "What will my mother say?"

So a mother who does the hard work of encouraging a girl to express her feelings, who accepts and adds to what she says, enables her daughter to identify her own desire, and to feel that it is a legitimate part of her. But, like all mother/daughter conversations, this one is difficult to choreograph. Lisette, like many mothers, finds that being open with her daughter Anna involves a step forward and then a step back. "I never know how much she wants to say, because it varies from one conversation to the next. And then, sometimes, she doesn't want me to say anything. I think we're having a good talk, and suddenly she turns on me and says, 'Why do you keep going on about this? I know that already!'"

## What She Doesn't Know

Few teenagers know precisely what they are doing, or what they are feeling in the sexual arena. Providing clear information is not enough to obliterate risk taking in sex. "I'm not stupid" and "I'd never let that happen" can be sincerely meant when uttered, but many teens come to learn that they do some of the stupid things they thought only stupid people did.[3] The areas of the teenage brain that are not yet awoken to fear and forward planning block the common-sense realization: "This is dangerous" or "This could happen to me!"

"Kids grow up so fast these days," many mothers reflect ruefully. "They're like teenagers by the time they're eleven. And by the age of twelve they have a sexual savvy that is quite unsettling." But in fact, kids are still kids, with a superficial knowledge of adult passions and complications. They confuse us and they confuse themselves with their sexy and savvy appearance. Looks are misleading.

The myth that children grow up fast is nowhere more entrenched than in ideas of what they know and do not know about sex. "Sexual messages are all around them," mothers remark. "You turn on the TV, and within five minutes someone's having sex. I flicked through the glossy magazine she's reading, and its more porn than fashion. It's all over the place."

But whatever exposure they have to sex in the mass media, whatever education parents and teachers give them, many American teenagers are startlingly ignorant of the most elementary facts of the human body and human sexuality.[4] There are subconscious depths of sexual desire and pleasure that make real understanding hard to come by. Shadowing each conversation are niggling questions: "How successful will I be in saying what it is I feel?" "Do I know what I feel?" "Will I feel the same tomorrow?"

During the teenage years, sexual feelings are so ambiguous that, for a mother, finding the so-called right approach is a far more complex matter, Lisette finds, than correcting the reticence of her own mother. The most effective question we can ask as mothers speaking to daughters is: How can I encourage her to recognize her own desires, and differentiate, for example, situational stimulation (from a party atmosphere or the mellow effect of alcohol) from a personal attraction? How can I convince her that her assessment of her own desire is the key to any decision she makes about sexual activity?

"I know that already!" is seldom a statement of fact. It is a gesture to bat away warnings, information, advice that are all too familiar but which do not suit them. Kasia, who got pregnant at sixteen, said, "My boyfriend and I had sex a few times, and nothing happened, so we thought it was okay," and then adds, "I never thought it would happen to me." And Meg, who became pregnant at seventeen, said, "I was drinking. He was drinking. I can't remember every little detail. I know you're always supposed to use a condom, but maybe this one time we just didn't."[5] But Meg's mother, Karen, says,

"You have no idea how many times I told her loud and clear that you have to use a condom, and a brand-new condom, every time you have intercourse. You have no idea how many times I told her alcohol messes with your judgment. What she says now is pathetic. She did know, because I told her over and over again."

However self-righteous teenage girls feel when they complain that a mother does not listen to them, or hear what they are trying to say, they, too, often fail to hear what their mothers say. Lisette, who values openness, notices that her daughter Anna is "out to lunch when I try to talk. I'm telling her when I'll be home and ask whether she'll be home when her sister gets back, and then I'll say, 'Anna?' and she goes: 'Oh, what was that?' She's in her own world half the time." It is not simply that girls do not listen in the sense of not taking things on board; in some sense, they simply do not hear. "I know she's talking, but what's going on in my head is much more real than anything she's saying," Anna explains. "And we get into these arguments: 'I told you I was going to pick you up and you just moseyed along with your friends,' and I think, 'Oh, no, was I supposed to hear something?'"

It can be hard enough getting a teenager's attention when we speak about practical, neutral details. When girls do not like a maternal message, their deafness increases. On the topic of sexual desire, about which girls themselves barely know what they think and feel, they can be particularly slow to process our input. And so, like Karen, we remain outraged by their ignorance of what we have told them, over and over.

## Why Girls Don't Listen

Abbey says that she herself benefits from conversations with her daughter Miri. "We talk about feelings in general," she explains. "You know, when you wonder whether physical attraction signals a deep attachment, or a flirtation? And how you can tell whether what you feel is friendship, or love? She's only seventeen, but she's not jaded, the way so many of my friends are, and I really like hearing her fresh ideas."

But sex talk is often difficult. Abbey sometimes finds Miri "really moody, and I never know whether we're going to have a real conversation, or whether she's going to hit the roof and tell me, 'I know that already!'"

While teenage girls value a mother's willingness to talk openly about sex, they can be irritated by sex talk. Miri says, "She talks about this stuff, and it makes me squirm. She's tells me what sex is, and what it's supposed to mean, like I can't figure it out for myself. She's so smug about her own sexuality, and gives me this stupid advice." She mimics: "'It's part of a whole relationship.' 'You have to be careful with yourself.' 'Sex has a serious emotional side.' I know all that stuff already."

Sex talk is problematic because it is intimate, and such intimacy involves dilemmas about both privacy and loyalty. "How much does she really want to know? My experience of sex is also about her stepfather, and I guess about her father," Abbey reflects. She finds that talking about sex is a matter of testing the waters, each time a conversation begins. "I take the cue from her. There are times she wants to ask something, and then she'll listen, and there are other times when she gets annoyed with me and tells me that I talk about sex too much!"

Confused about her own feelings, a daughter experiences a mother's voice as stronger than her own, and it threatens to interfere with her half-formed feelings. "Mothers and sex don't go together," Miri tells me. While we readily see the truth of what she says, mothers are sexual beings; and most mothers of teenage girls are sexually active. But a daughter's sexual feelings, especially when they are charged with confusion, are private, and exposure to a mother's eyes can arouse shame and rage. Miri says she feels her mother's words "like fingers inside me trying to rearrange my thoughts." A mother offers her view or her advice, aiming for a rational exchange. Yet as she speaks, she registers deep concern about a daughter's well-being, fear for her vulnerability and uncertainty, perhaps, at her own position as adviser. A daughter responds to these layers, particularly during sex talk when what is discussed is also intimate and internal.

So the modern mom comes up against unexpected rejections. "I'm doing everything that my mom didn't and should have," Lisette says, "and my daughter complains about my openness as vehemently as I complained about my own mother's reticence."

## Back to the Intimate History

A mother's body is our first home, and many psychoanalytic theorists believe that this fact becomes central to our emotional makeup.[6] In our infancy, a mother's smell, feel, voice, and touch pervade our senses. She is, or is experienced as being, our source of food, warmth, safety, and comfort. She is our world, and becomes closely identified with our self.

This intimacy is shared. A mother is likely to feel as intimately connected with her infant as her dependent infant is with her. A mother is both self and child. This tension between mother/child as a special unit, and mother/child as two different people responding to each other in an interpersonal way, forms the bedrock of the parent/child relationship. While boys, at the close of infancy, have a different gender identity that enforces self-boundaries, girls do not. While a boy's gender difference reminds a mother that her child is distinct from her, she may continue to identify profoundly with a daughter.[7]

As a daughter matures, a mother is far more aware of a girl's physical development than any other family member. Fathers often say they are surprised by a sudden realization that a daughter has, for example, been wearing a bra or menstruating for a long time. They are surprised because they have not noticed the small signs of intermediate growth. Girls themselves notice their breast development at age eleven or twelve, but a mother notices it at ten. She notices the small skin problems her daughter hopes only she can see as she peers into the mirror. She notices even a few pounds' weight gain. She may learn tact and she may learn tolerance, but she never learns blindness. This watchful caring can be experienced as an intrusive "knowing" to a girl who tries to keep her mother at bay with the charge, "You don't have a clue who I really am!"

This identification is tested during adolescence by both mother and daughter. Across a range of issues, teenage girls utter frequent identity reminders while shopping, driving, talking: "I know how to get there myself," or "I'm perfectly capable of doing this myself," "I'm not stupid, you know," and "I know what I'm doing!" These sharp reminders hone a girl's own sense of competence. These reminders need an extra edge when the discussion is about sex—a topic about blurred boundaries, and about which girls can rarely say, "I know what I feel."

## Mother Knows Best?

It is difficult for a mother to keep calm when she is trying to work with her daughter on a subject as important as sex, when she may face a daughter's moodiness for being intrusive, and when she has to break through that infuriating adolescent deafness. It is difficult to send the message that a daughter is a strong young woman when, in regard to her sexuality, she may well be unaware of her own vulnerability. Bridget says of her fifteen-year-old daughter, Cassie, "She thinks she's strong. And I guess in some ways she is. She has guts. But she doesn't know how much it can hurt to be dumped by someone she thinks she's in love with, let alone someone she's had sex with. She doesn't realize how delicate her confidence is. I do. I've been there. And I thought I knew everything, but it's not that easy. You're far more vulnerable than you think. The feelings involved in sex are far deeper than you think. I hope she means it when she says, 'I know what I'm doing and I'm in charge.' But I know from experience how suddenly all that can change, and you're stunned at your own stupidity."

Girls claim that they know what they are doing, partly out of pride, and partly from being unable to name the pressures on them. Bridget believes that her daughter, Cassie, is more influenced by her boyfriend than she admits, or perhaps realizes. "She has this cute, bright manner when she's with him. She's nervous about pleasing him and smoothing everything over. He suggests something, you know, about where they're going to go, and she falls over saying what a good idea that is. And then she tells me where they're going, and just about falls apart when I say 'no.' And it's not that she wants to go to that club or that party, it's that she doesn't know how to tell him she can't. So what am I to think about what she's like when she's alone with him? I have good reasons for worrying, but she thinks I'm worrying because I'm a stupid old mother."

Cassie says precisely what her mother predicts she will say: "No one tells me what to do. I can think for myself. I do what I want to do. No one is going to make me do what I don't want to do."

But Bridget persists: "I see you with this guy. I see what you're like. You can't even begin to say what you want to do and what you don't. And I wasn't born yesterday. I know what it's like to be fifteen."

And Cassie says, "You don't have any idea what it's like to be me."

Bridget remembers clearly what it was like being Cassie's age. She remembers what it was like not knowing what it was she wanted to do. She now wants Cassie to focus on the centrality of her own wishes, and not be swayed by those of her boyfriend. "I know she's putting on a front. I know how difficult it is to say something that's going to put a friendship in danger. And I can see how Cassie's changed since she started going out with this guy, but it began with her girlfriends first. She gets into a panic when I tell her she can't do something her friends are doing. She loses it. She becomes totally irrational, and just argues and argues, and then starts screaming at me. She cannot accept that she sometimes has to say, 'I can't go. My mom won't let me.' For her, that would be the worst thing in the world."

Bridget wants to protect her daughter from pressure that

will cloud her judgment, and from the varieties of unhappiness that arise from being under someone else's thumb. She wants to get across the message: "You are too important to play second fiddle to anyone"; but the message Cassie hears is: "You cannot look after yourself." Cassie spurns the protection, which stems from love, and interprets her mother's position as one of control, which she bizarrely attributes to meanness: "Mom is set on ruining my social life. I tell her I'm going out and I get the third degree, with 'no you're not.' I might as well forget about having a life until I leave home."

Cassie's increasing opposition sparks Bridget to make a more extreme statement: "Tony exploits you. He calls you, and you drop everything. He calls all the shots. You think he's so special. I'd like to know what he gives you that's so special."

"You don't know what you're talking about."

"For one thing, you drop everything to see him. And you see him every day."

"So what! I see you every day. You see Dad every day."

"That's in the course of my life! I'm not the one who's messing everything around to see him. I'm not the one who's dropping courses and getting bad grades!"

Bridget denigrates what Tony "gives" Cassie. She wants to overpower her daughter's current distractions for her future good. It seems important now, but other things are more important for her future.

Bridget says, "I have a choice. I can take things easy, give myself an easy life, and let this boy exploit her, or I can have my say."

"You just want me to stay your little girl forever. You have your own hang-ups about guys, and you're laying them on me."

"Anyone in her right mind would have hang-ups about this guy."

"See—you have hang-ups."

"You stay with that attitude and you'll have lots to be sorry for."

"There is no point talking to you. You don't know him. You don't know me. There's nothing more to say."

Cassie hurls at her mother the familiar charge that she is holding her back ("You just want me to stay your little girl forever"). Bridget admits to having hang-ups but says in regard to Cassie's boyfriend Tony, they are justified. Cassie then uses what's called the Aikido approach.[8] Taken from the martial art of using an opponent's force against him, in conversation it involves taking someone's words and using them to force a contradiction. So when Bridget admits to "hang-ups" about Cassie's boyfriend, Cassie points out that this admission supports her argument and undermines her mother's. Seeking a shortcut to her point, Bridget then falls into the threatening pattern of "You'll be sorry," which Cassie cannot contradict with any certainty, so she makes a move of total rejection: "You don't know me. There's nothing more to say."

A mother's tendency to be watchful of her daughter's interactions with men makes sense to a mother and is senseless to a daughter. Teenage girls admit doubts on many fronts, but can panic at being excluded by a friend or a boyfriend, which makes it impossible for them to key in to the justified concern of a mother. They resent the infliction of fear, and find that a mother's fear can interfere with their own sense of adventure, autonomy, and initiative. Bridget faces the ultimate maternal question: Is *this* the time to refuse to negotiate and to say, "I don't care what you think you feel. This isn't right for you"? Or, is this a time to let her daughter live and learn? We stand on this border as we watch our daughters move into the sexual arena.

## What Can We Do When We're "Too Late"?

Sometimes a girl's sexual awareness strikes early, simply because of her internal body clock. Gemma, at fifteen, has the body of a mature woman. She was first among her peers to menstruate and the first to experience the kick of hormonal moodiness. By the time she was thirteen, she was fitted for a D-cup bra. A sexually mature woman among a cohort of kids, she became a sex object even among friends and teachers. Teachers' eyes lingered on her body, not because they had inappropriate desires, but because it is natural to observe these changes. The boys in her class taunted her about her breasts and set up a betting system among themselves to see who could "score." Even girls would chastise her for "showing too much," if she happened to wear a top that suddenly, without her noticing it, had become tightfitting.

Gemma describes her ambivalence about her rapid development: "It changed my life, because it changed my relationship with everyone. Even my grandmother started giving my mom a hard time about how I looked and shouldn't I cover up. Guys from school would come up to talk to me, and I thought we were having a genuine conversation, and then I'd see the same guy gesturing and laughing with his friends. Every day there'd be some betrayal like that."

She half wants to talk to her mother about it, but then gets easily "put off, because she gets so concerned and she probably wants to ask a hundred questions, but she doesn't dare to. I think she's scared to know the whole truth. She'd probably like me still to be a virgin, even though she knows I'm not."

She has been sexually active for about a year. While her mother, Robyn, says she would have much preferred this not to have happened, she understands that her daughter's physical development was probably part of a hormonal kick, which made sex seem necessary. "She would have been a Juliet pursuing her Romeo in another day and age. I can live with this." Robyn is relieved that Gemma has told her about her sexual activity and taken her advice, as far as she can tell, about birth control. But she is in a quandary about the emotional roller coaster her daughter now rides. She asks what she thinks is a neutral question:

Robyn: "You're not seeing Jed tonight?"

Gemma: "I guess not! I said I was going to be home."

Robyn: "Well, that's nice. So am I."

There is a pause during which Gemma looks at her mother to assess whether there is some other meaning in what she says. She can see that her mother is thinking about what to say.

Gemma: "You might as well say it. I can't stand it when you sort of half say things."

Robyn: "I just wanted to know what's up. That sort of thing."

Gemma: "You wanted to know if he dumped me."

Robyn: "I want to know whatever you want to tell me."

Gemma: "You want to know more than that!"

After another pause, Gemma adds: "You think I'm a slut!"

Robyn: "I don't!"

After a stunned pause, she asks: "Why?"

Gemma: "Because I probably am. Because that's probably what everyone thinks, and you must have heard it."

Robyn: "No one's saying that, and no one would dare say that around me."

Gemma: "So much for what you know."

Robyn: "What's going on, Gem!"

Gemma: "You're stupid. That's what's going on. You don't know anything."

Many mothers know that there is a lot about a teenage daughter's life they do not know. The daily dramas of life with friends are glimpsed only in part. Not seeing the broad context, it is easy to strike the wrong note. Robyn initially thinks she is offering comfort to Gemma, and then discovers that Gemma links her mother's guess that something has gone wrong in her relationship with Jed to her reputation as "a slut." While Robyn is innocent of having made any accusation, the conversation almost proceeds as though she had.

Repeatedly mothers say that a daughter "is all over the place" when talking about an actual sexual relationship—denying it one moment, then saying something the next that seems to contradict the denial ("I would never do that" and then "I only did that once"). Robyn says, "I don't know where I am with her. I don't know where she is. And when she says things like that—about her terrible reputation—I panic. In one of her foul moods she told me she was refered to by one guy as 'the community chest.' I guess that means the chest everyone puts something in. It's horrible! I'd do anything to protect her from this. I don't think she's doing much to protect herself!"

Mothers like Robyn, Lisette, and Abbey reflect carefully about how to be open, supportive, and informative when discussing sex with a daughter. Then they come up against a daughter's confusion and their own maternal fears. Robyn is hurt as deeply as her daughter by the taunts of her peers. Each trying to protect the other, their anger increases; they quarrel, and greater understanding, however painful, can be a consequence of the quarrel.

## In a Minefield, Try a Variety of Routes

Mothers want to improve their role in leading their daughters to a deeper knowledge of sex and good sense, and many writers and educators now offer encouragement and guidelines.[9] The girls in my study express strong views as to why these efforts so often founder. "Mothers and sex don't go together" is a statement with some truth, but it is one we can work against as we try to talk to them. The aims are to:

- Encourage sensual awareness.
- Emphasize sexual entitlement.

To do this we can:

- Key into 'I'm not ready' messages (which are often difficult to distinguish from 'It's too late, so I don't want to hear you' messages).
- Admit to being confused yourself sometimes.
- Ask if they want to hear about your experiences before actually relating them.
- Assess your own comfort level—not only is this your right, but trying to disguise your unease is impossible with your hawk-eyed daughter.
- Emphasize difference—in sexual responses, in levels of desire or need, and in sexual orientation

Sexual pleasure is one aspect of self-knowledge and personal power. While parents and teachers emphasize restraint in the teen years, adolescence offers opportunity for a broader discussion of feelings. This is a time when young people want to process their experience and put it in a wider human context: "Which of my experiences are shared by others and which are unique to me?" they ask. "How do I handle my sexual feelings when they seem at odds with my emotional bond to someone?" they wonder. And so, when we want a good conversation, we should bear in mind that we are helping a daughter explore her own feelings.

Girls may be taken in by the way desire is sold—as something that others like or expect, which they should have. They may also misread others' desire for them, seeing it as more of an attachment than it turns out to be, or more of a commitment, or a deeper emotional bond. The momentary desire of someone they care for may seem so urgent that they believe they are causing harm or real hurt by refusing to grant what is desired. They could be encouraged to focus on the question: "What does my body want to feel and allow me to do?" And we can help focus on this by showing a willingness to hear her speak about a range of desires.

We can also admit that sexual feelings are often confusing for everyone. It may comfort her to know that adults are confused, too, about what they feel and for whom. It may be easier for her to reflect on her own feelings when she is not intimidated by the expectation that mature adults glide easily through their own sexuality.

Above all, we can assure her that she does not have to choose between being a sexual being and an acceptable daughter. We can encourage her to be active in shaping her own sexual encounters, and we can reassure her that no one gets it right every time.

# 11.

## *"So that's how you feel!":*
## *How Conflict Can Lead*
## *to Closeness*

**MORE QUARRELS** occur between a teenage daughter and mother than between any parent-child pair, and these quarrels wound more deeply as the daughter sheds her resilient childhood skin and as mothers become newly sensitive to a daughter's words. The same words, uttered with the same vehemence and pitch, will make a different impact on a parent, depending on whether the daughter is five or fifteen. "I hate you" means one thing when a tired five-year-old screams it than it does when shouted by a moody fifteen-year-old. "You stink" is just a silly phrase, when uttered by a four-year-old. We correct her manners, but do not worry about her character.

When she reaches adolescence, her insults are more painful. A child has intense moments of anger, but these are not seen as integrated into that larger cluster of responses and reflections we generally call "our feeling for someone." "Go away!" or "You're awful!" means one thing when it is uttered by a child who is trying to use a pair of scissors and is resisting a mother's help and another thing when uttered by a teenager who feels her mother is interfering with her life. "I'm not mad now," a child will announce a moment after the peak of her tantrum. Her proud determination to mean what she says in anger is soon forgotten. The rift with her mother is quickly and seamlessly mended. Conflict intensifies in the teenage years not only because daughters become more oppositional, but also because mothers feel that opposition more acutely. These rifts, even when repaired, leave fault lines.

A mother's new sensitivity is matched by that of her daughter, who is quick to read criticisms into every comment. A suggestion, a correction, a word of sympathy may spark emotional fireworks: "Leave me alone!" "Stop trying to run my life for me," "You're always telling me what to do," "You don't understand!" and "You don't know anything!" In search of a mother's constructive responsiveness, a teenage girl often becomes newly vulnerable to any sign that what she is doing isn't right. In an adolescent plagued by self-consciousness, a mother's passing comment about her posture, her hair, her voice, can set off panic as she realizes, for the hundredth time that day, that someone is watching and assessing her. A causal criticism, which once may have been a passing correction, such as pushing the hair away from her eyes or brushing something off her sweater, will be experienced as an assault. She will be reluctant to forgive someone who humiliates her—and no one can humiliate her as easily as a parent from whom she expects admiration.

## New Power to Wound

A vivid picture of a daughter's new power to wound her mother appears in the diary Anne Frank kept from 1941 to 1944, charting her typical teenage development amid extraordinary and tragic events. In the entry of October 14, 1942, she is lying in bed, waiting for her father to come to join her in their customary evening prayers. Her mother asks whether she can say the prayers with her tonight. Anne declines, insisting she wants her father, not her mother. Her mother hesitates, considering whether to argue the point, and then leaves saying, "Love cannot be forced." Anne hears her crying throughout the night.

Anne is a teenager, presenting a teen's characteristic self-righteousness. She is also a consummate observer who describes the situation from both her own and her mother's side. She notes her mother's pain, and the reason for it: Her mother now takes this preference for her father as a sign that Anne does not love her.

What could be more familiar than a child's refusal to let anyone else, even another parent, step in and take over someone else's tried and tested routine. "I want a story from Daddy," a five-year-old demands. "No! Daddy!" she insists when her mother offers to read to her instead, because her father is tied up elsewhere. "I want Mommy/Sister/Daddy/Nanna," a hurt child will proclaim, seeking at that moment comfort from one person only, convinced at that moment that no one else will do. Usually parents take this in their stride. The child's proclaimed preference may be inconvenient. It may be embarrassing. But it is not deeply wounding. It would be met with, at worst, a gruff "Tough!" but it would not make anyone cry half the night.

What Anne's mother felt, and what mothers of many adolescent girls feel, is that a daughter's declaration of preferences and her rejections take on new meanings. As her mother registers a profound insult, Anne sees that her battle to be considered an individual person, powerfully aware of her own mind, is won. With a teen's cruelty, she savors this, listening to her mother cry throughout the night.

## Changing Emotional Weather

The anger at a mother can set in like a fog, so that it seems to be the stable air; but emotional weather is changeable. We know this is true with a child, and sometimes forget it is also true of a teenage daughter. As Carol Gilligan says, writing about her own mother, "The anger between mothers and daughters is legendary; the love is often held in silence."[1] Teens broadcast their criticisms; mothers speak out about problems; few highlight the love that informs both the criticisms and the problems.

Anne's *Diary* has often been read as a typical mother/teenage daughter story. The daughter rejects the practical, sensible woman who criticizes and misunderstands her, and doesn't know who she really is. The teenage girl then turns to her father who, less involved, less familiar, receives fewer complaints. Anne writes, "Daddy is always so nice to me, and he understands me so much better too. Oh, I can't stand Mummy at such times, and I am a stranger as far as she is concerned as well, for you see, she doesn't even know how I think about the most ordinary things." Anne, arch and distant, reports that her mother accuses her of making herself out to be a grand lady.

Anne's negative pronouncements on her mother and their relationship are stamped on generations of readers' memories. Unnoticed are other entries that show connection as playful and profound as that between a young child and her mother. In an entry also written on October 14, 1942, Ann writes: "Mummy, Margot and I are as thick as thieves again. It's really much better. I get into Margot's bed now almost every evening."[2]

The adolescent anger that seems like a permanent feature of the landscape blocks out a girl's (and woman's) knowledge of her love for her mother, only when she cannot find her way back. When she does find her way back to her mother, she falls silent. After all, why analyze something that is problem-free? This silence, however, means that the positive connection is ignored.

Here is how fourteen-year-old Kirsty and her mother, Judith, move through the conflict and to a new closeness.

Kirsty describes a recent quarrel during which she "got tired of making my case, and just wanted to push her away. I said something like, 'Go away! I hate you. I really hate you!' I'm sure I've said stuff like that before. When I was saying it I was just thinking about how angry I was and how this was just another fight. But when I saw her face, I guess then I realized what I'd said. For half a second I was even angrier. Like: 'You're not going to lay that on me, are you? You're not going to try to make me feel guilty for being angry when you're the one who's being so unreasonable?' But I didn't say that because she really was hurt, and she was even trying to hide it, not to lay on the guilt, and I really felt bad."

Judith admits the quarreling with Kirsty has worn her down. "You think that you have something permanent with your child. All that time, all that involvement. Then she throws it your face. Yeah, I feel bruised, and I'm worried, because if it gets worse then I don't know what's going to happen, and I'm worried because once she makes up her mind about something, my say doesn't count for anything. And the way she lashes out at me. This 'I hate you' stuff— well, it really stuns me."

As Judith broods on her daughter's verbal slap, Kirsty discovers that her remarks now have a different meaning to her mother. At twelve, she could tell her mother that she hated her, and Judith saw a sulky, moody kid, in the throes, perhaps, of hormonal edginess. Judith would have greeted her daughter's declaration, at the age of eight, "I hate you" as a sign she had had a rough day at school, probably had been teased in the playground or excluded from a more popular girl's party. At the age of four, a declaration, "I hate you," would have indicated a tired or hungry child, one worn out by the simple demands of living and growing.

Suddenly, at sixteen, the words mean something different. Kirsty has been struggling to make her mother see her as "a real person and not just her daughter, not that little girl she thinks she knows." Yet the realization that her mother does see her as an independent person who knows her own mind comes as a shock.

## Recovery

Why do so many mothers and daughters get to this low point and then recover a good relationship?

The usual explanation is that a teen "matures" or "gets over adolescence" or passes through a "phase." What this explanation leaves out is the process by which she passes through this phase, and what she learns from these negative interactions. For a girl's experience of her new powers in hurting her mother can actually offer the recognition she is seeking. The new pain she can inflict (using the same words she used as a child, which then did not strike deep) shows her that her mother is responding to her in new ways. The mother's shocked sense of rejection assures the daughter that her mother "takes her seriously." She accepts that the daughter knows her own mind, and is not "just tired" or "just in a bad mood." The mother and daughter, now probably able to stand shoulder to shoulder, are now able to look at each other eye to eye as people. A daughter who may have been overstating her case, and saying more than she felt, because she expects she won't be heard, now sees that her mother is listening. Seeing this, and aware that she has hurt her mother, she now takes new care, and feels a new responsibility for what she says.

"I'm a lot more careful. Not that I'm always nice to her. You mustn't think that!" Kirsty laughs. "But I did do a double take when I saw her face. Usually there's this weary mask, like she's pretending she knows what I'm doing and she's not going to be taken in. But this time it was—Wham! I really got her there. And for a minute I thought, 'Ha! Serves you right.' But it was also scary because I don't want—I mean, it's not right, is it?—for her to think I really hate her. I felt so— oh, so unsettled afterwards. But I wasn't going to cave in. No way. I was pleased she was suffering. (Am I mean? Too bad!) But I was also sorry."

Being "a lot more careful" with a mother can be inhibiting. Teenage girls who treat a mother with great care and consideration because they see her as weak miss out on certain things, and may suppress useful parts of the relationship. But taking care, in the way Kirsty means, is part of seeing a mother in a new light, as a real person with feelings. It is also a way of seeing herself in another light vis-à-vis her mother, as someone whose responses have the stature and meaning of a distinct, different person. Learning of her power to hurt, she gains the recognition she craves.

Kirsty shifts from seeing her mother as someone "who is

always so sure of herself she never bothers to see my point of view" to someone who can be "rattled and made to stop and think and come off that high horse of hers." Sometimes it's a matter of pride: We don't want to show a daughter she has hurt us. "You're not going to that party. I don't care what you think of me" can be a reasonable line for a mother to take; but persisting in saying that a daughter's love (or hatred) is a matter of indifference ("I don't care how you feel") is an insult to the power of her feelings. When a teen's hostility is minimized, or interpreted as a child's tantrum, then she feels discounted. Acknowledging a teenager's anger is part of acknowledging her. Sometimes we try to ignore an angry daughter because we don't know what else to do. But ignoring her seldom puts the problem to bed. Instead, she raises the ante. If we appear to have superior protection against her anger, our teen tries to become a superior attacker.

As we begin to discern the outlines of this complex and passionate connection, we will be less hurt by the critical and irritable blows against us. As we tolerate the (basically inconsequential, unserious) attacks, we may be less inclined to counterattack with accusations about bad attitude or ingratitude. And, in the midst of a heated battle, we may be less terrified that a daughter will reject our love and protection. There is, in this sense, a very strong link between understanding the relationship and improving it.

## Exposing Ourselves to Our Daughters

Girls want to get to know a mother, using their new abilities to explore a familiar person. The new power girls have to understand a mother is often a delight. "I didn't realize that you had a life," Kirsty says to her mother, Judith, who has been stewing over a tiff she has just had with a female friend. "That happens to me all the time, Mom." Kirsty can offer comfort and understanding, and she also takes pleasure in catching sight of this new dimension. "You sometimes get the idea that life as you know it stops, maybe around thirty or so. It's kind of cool to see that it goes on, pretty much the same. My mom's funny. She gets really upset by some cutting remark from a girlfriend, and she worries about being excluded. Sometimes she gets upset about things and I think, 'That's just stupid,' but I understand. It's kind of cool."

But girls sometimes say they feel rebuffed when they try to get to know a mother. Carol Gilligan recalls that, as a teen, she eventually gave up on getting to know her mother, and turned away, frozen out by her mother's refusal to open up to her. She now realizes that her mother was trying, with her reserve, to protect Carol from old family griefs. In addition, her mother saw her duty as training Carol to become a good acceptable woman, someone who would behave properly, and be beyond social reproach. To do this job, the mother believed she had to present herself as a perfect role model.

Looking back at her adolescence, and her changing relationship with her mother, the mature psychologist now sees a broader picture, and a common pattern in this breach. To protect her daughter's future as a woman in society, Carol's mother allied herself with society's view of womanhood. It was at this time that her pragmatic mother began to control and criticize her, to speak and direct without listening for her daughter's response.[3] While the teenage Carol wanted to use her new powers of understanding to engage with the complexities of her mother's life, her mother turned her socially acceptable face to Carol, and covered the rest.

It is not easy for a woman to be known so well by someone who is often arch, supercilious, and critical, and whose high standards are as yet untested. Teenage girls use their razor-sharp perception to criticize from a new vantage point. A daughter still sees the mother who was once beyond criticism, a mother who defined normality, whose worldview was tantamount to knowledge and truth. She also sees a woman living in the world the teen herself is rapidly coming to understand. This woman may be ordinary or "typical." She is a woman with some limitations and some weaknesses who may have made a wrong decision here and there, taken too many, or too few, risks. But understanding one's mother's rough edges, regrets, and confusions helps a daughter negotiate her own womanhood. Instead of using some unworkable ideal in which everything should be assured, controlled, and correct, she accepts that her own uncertainties are legitimate.

Mothers frequently describe a tension between wanting to be honest with their daughters and wanting to protect them from their problems, anxieties, and complications. Believing that they should appear to be the parent in charge, the parent who can contain all danger, they decline to open up to them.

An important step in authorizing a daughter—encouraging her to speak her own mind, to know her own heart—is to engage with what she says, even when it's hard to hear. But this becomes increasingly difficult as her words and insights challenge us. Just as daughters need mothers to be more open and intimate with them, daughters become capable of wounding mothers more deeply than ever before.

## Reserve and Hypocrisy

Teenage girls have a sharp vision: they see a lot, they want to see more. Not telling them things is, in their view, like lying.

Allie, at eighteen, explains, "When I heard Mom had been married before, you know, before she married my dad, I was like—you know, just shaking my head. As a kid, I'd heard a lot about this guy she was engaged to and how awful he was, and why even smart women did stupid things. And when she told me and I said she should've told me before—and that's a mild version of what I said—she said she wasn't lying, she had been engaged to him, that bit was true, she just hadn't added the fact that they were married, and it wasn't my business anyway, and she told me because she thought I was so stuck on Scott, and she wanted to say that sometimes you do make a real mistake when you're young, and she was telling me you know to give me permission to mess up and move on. But what I feel—I don't know whether I'm just angry, but what I feel is—well, I'm so disillusioned, and not because she was married before, but because that was so not part of what she told me about herself, and its that that gets me."

Personal privacy may be a right we take for granted, but it will nonetheless be challenged by a teenage daughter. Allie feels the weight of past secrets. She says, "I now understand why it's sometimes so hard to talk to my mom. There are these things you're just not supposed to say."

We consciously and unconsciously censor ourselves as we try to fit in with our families and friends. We try to figure out what will bring us love and approval. We discover at a very early age that people who love us can disapprove of what we say and do, and their cold and critical responses can shatter our sense that the relationship is secure. So we may decide to censor or silence certain impulses and thoughts. Psychological theory reminds us that what is censored becomes distorted, and, ultimately, gets blown out of proportion. Undisclosed, it finds its way into our psyche, and returns in a disguised, obtrusive form.

When mothers censor aspects of themselves, teenage daughters respond by being less open. Feeling excluded, a teen begins to hide her own thoughts and perhaps lies about her own activities. However much she wants to open up, she feels that honesty is squeezed out of the relationship if it is not mutual.

A girl's inability to speak out to a mother is usually accompanied by her belief that her mother does not open up to her. Steph, sixteen, says she is "fed up with my mom telling me everything's fine between her and my dad. Then why does she get that funny look when he says something to her, like about where he's going. I mean, a kid could see something's up. Why does she think I don't see it, at my age? It's really disillusioning, you know, this sort of thing, when they think they can tell you anything and expect you to believe it."

The disillusion is not about a mother having problems. It is about her withholding information. Steph knows enough to see that the superficial information her mother gives her is inadequate, and she feels betrayed. "We still are okay a lot of the time, but this is always between us. And sometimes she asks, 'Well, tell me how things are,' and I look at her and I think: Why should I tell you anything?"

## The Burden of Knowing

Steph's mother, Delia, is circumspect when she speaks to me, but knows her not telling is relevant to her relationship with her daughter. "It's not fair to dump all this onto your child. The way I feel—well, it's a kind of permanent nausea, a sort of dread at anything happening at all. She has her own life. I don't want her to stay in because I'm lonely. I don't want her worrying about me."

While mothers explain they do not want to burden a daughter with their problems, or feel they should protect a daughter from adult ambiguities, daughters complain that their mothers are not honest and open with them. Jenny says, "Senka sees me with one boyfriend followed by another, and when she asks what happened to Mike, I give as calm and uninformative an answer as possible. Sometimes she gets huffy, you know, 'Whatever,' she says and walks away in kind of disgust. I guess to her I'm a woman who can't keep things going with a man, but explaining what really happened, supposing I could, isn't going to make things better."

But Senka has wide-ranging complaints about her mother's reticence. "I heard from a friend's mother when your jewelery show got that write-up in the paper. I heard from [my older brother] when you had that cancer scare. You don't tell *me* anything."

A mother's urge to protect comes into conflict with the relational imperative to be authentic. In many mother/daughter pairs at least one member wants to cushion the other from criticism and pain and anger. Usually the mother is the more protective one as she mutes the intensity of her dissatisfaction and need. However, a daughter—even a very young one—is tuned in to a mother's feelings. So while a mother feels she is protecting her daughter, she may be allowing inauthenticity to enter the relationship. "Nothing's wrong" may be said to protect a daughter, but if the daughter sees clearly that something is wrong, the intended protection becomes an obvious lie, and hence something that creates distance between her and her mother. She feels, "My mother doesn't trust me," or "My mother doesn't want to talk to me."

Empathy for someone who is unhappy, especially if we love that person, is painful. Delia wants to protect Steph from the intensity of her feelings, but Steph is nonetheless aware of her mother's state. A tension then arises between authenticity and sensitivity to the other. Unspoken or unrepresented feelings can create frustrating gaps in a relationship. Some researchers have noticed a correlation between a mother's reluctance to lay her problems open to a daughter's view and a daughter's willingness to lie to her mother.[4] Openness involves making oneself vulnerable. Why should a daughter expose herself if a mother does not?

Outside a context of mutual honesty, Steph refuses to take the risk involved in being honest with her mother. She explains why she is not going to tell her mother about an abortion she has scheduled next week. "I've been going through all this, and she doesn't know a thing. I look at her and think: 'You are so stupid not to know.' But then maybe she does, and just doesn't say anything. And even though it's sometimes right on the tip of my tongue and I really want to tell her and just have it out there and see what she'd do with it, I don't want it between us forever. I want to do it and get it over with. It's bad enough with my doctor, who makes me go through this counseling thing. But that's okay. I can step away from that. I couldn't from her. And then it would be with her now. She'd think, 'This is my grandchild,' and it would be another thing for her to carry around. And then she'd worry about me afterwards. You know, I can feel her creeping around wondering whether she should say something, whether she shouldn't. And that's how it would be with this. I'd rather just go through it. I can go with a friend. It will be fine. If she doesn't know, I can forget it."

Not telling a mother is part protection of the relationship, part protection of the mother, and part protection of herself, because involving her mother would be to engage with this in a very different way. And Steph believes she can get away with this because "Mom's so caught up in her own deception, she won't see what's going on with me."

Daughters normally unload a lot on their mothers. They dump on them when they are in a bad mood. They often blame them for their own unhappiness. But they also, at times, protect a mother from their own painful or confusing experiences, such as unsettling sexual episodes, tiffs with friends, anxiety about grades or being bullied. In doing so, they protect themselves against a mother's anxiety ("Oh, my God, are you all right?") or anger ("I told you so") or sympathy ("I hate it when she feels sorry for me"), but they are also protecting a mother from worry.

Mothers and daughters, getting to know one another anew, risk burdening one another with brutal honesty on the one hand, and falling into superficiality on the other. In a vigorous relationship, these alternatives are constantly tested. Each hopes to find authenticity safe, after all.

## Windows of Opportunity

Teenage girls are not always easy to talk to. But even when they are being difficult, there is often a window of opportunity in which they try to explain themselves, and mothers can learn to spot this opening.

Teenage girls say they hate it when people don't listen, but they can also be slow to speak out. Most mothers say they want to listen to their daughters, and most offer concessions for honesty. "I would rather know where she is, even if she's doing what I disapprove of, than have her lie to me" is a common sentiment.

So why do girls sometimes refuse to be open? Why is a slamming door or a shout in the form of "There's no point talking to you!" such a familiar move in mother/daughter arguments?

Often a quarrel erupts just as we are doing our utmost to understand our daughter. "Don't you see how dangerous this is?" we ask. "Why are you doing this to yourself?" "Can't you see where this is leading?"

These can be genuine questions, yet a daughter responds to them as a form of mockery or criticism.

Teens sometimes refuse to open up in the face of a parent's questions, because they themselves do not know the answers. Explaining how one feels or why something is important can be difficult. Articulating the pressures they face—from girlfriends, boyfriends, teachers, and parents—is not easy. Sometimes teens express fury at a parent's interest when they simply don't know how to explain themselves.

So closely bound is a daughter to her mother that she may blame her mother for her own internal confusion.

When we take on board the difficulty teens have of

explaining complex views and feelings, we can transform our exasperation at being blamed into patience. "Why is this so important to you?" can become "Can we find a way of talking about this?"

## So What Can Mothers and Daughters Do?

There may be common themes of anger and rejection as girls go through adolescence, but there are also ways of avoiding the serious rifts in relationships that so frequently occur between mother and daughter at this point in their lives. On the one hand, we don't want to burden a daughter with our personal problems, but on the other we don't want to "hide" them, thereby establishing a pattern of reserve that, with the teenager's high standards of honesty, will seem either dishonest or hypocritical.

When we have a difficult problem, we can avoid presenting it as a burden to a daughter by showing her that we can approach it positively. This doesn't mean being able to solve it. This doesn't mean we can always avoid feeling down about it. A daughter knows when a mother's assertion, "I'm fine," is not true, and, to a daughter, that untruth will be a lie and rejection, and may make her sufficiently angry to say, "I'll lie to you too!"

While we tell a daughter that, yes, some things are difficult, we can also say, "This is how I'm trying to think about it."

When she does engage with us, we can show her that she has the ability to comfort us. We can take in what she says about our problems, and think about her comments and suggestions.

When a daughter hurts us, we can tell her she has. Saying "That really hurt me" has more positive effect than "How dare you!" Showing her we are hurt sends the message: Your feelings are real and powerful.

The questions mothers must put to themselves are:

Can we be open and admit our ignorance, describe what we've given up, discuss our regrets, and lay ourselves open to a daughter's critical view? Or do we harden in the face of their criticism. "What do you know?" we might demand of a daughter as, with her untested ideals, she declares, "This is what you should have been!"

Do we follow the pragmatic path and tell her how she should behave, what she should say if she wants to be accepted and avoid criticism? Or do we risk allowing her to be open, individual, and vulnerable? To support a daughter in taking this risk, we must be open ourselves.

# 12.    *The Lifelong Dialogue*

**MOTHER AND TEENAGE DAUGHTER** often appear to occupy a battleground. For decades this vital opposition has been misinterpreted as a battle of wills whereby a daughter tries to push a mother away, and a mother refuses to let go. A closer look at these struggles reveals an intricate choreography whereby girls seek to change their position within this relationship, whereby mothers learn new steps in communication and response, and whereby both mother and daughter work hard to keep their love up-to-date.

Teenage girls may seem to push a mother away, but one of their greatest fears is being abandoned by her. Quick to complain about her intrusiveness and control, they also speak of their profound need for her love, understanding, and support. While girls talk freely about the ways the relationship pinches, their profound love and attachment are more likely to be expressed in conversational shifts, off-guard remarks, and codas of reflection than in up-front announcements. Above all, a fear of abandonment emerges in dreams and private musings or fears. Alex, age fifteen, who bounces arguments off her mother with ruthless confidence, describes a recurrent dream:

> I came home from school and the door to our house was locked. Maybe I had the key—I don't remember—but I still couldn't get in. Every time I tried the door, something was different about it. I looked around, to see if my mother was just behind me, but everything around our house was changed. There was just dust and dirt, and the kind of ridges you get when there's been some big machine moving in mud. I suddenly realized my mother and father weren't around here anywhere, and I was terrified. Then I wake up.

Gemma who, at fifteen, appears to her mother, Robyn, as "so grown up I feel totally thrown," confesses:

> Sometimes, when I'm walking home from school, or when I'm in my room and my mom is somewhere else, I suddenly feel afraid. I'm not afraid about anything in particular, but my heart starts pounding and I get dizzy. I sort of steady myself and go into the kitchen or the yard and wait for my mom. When she comes in, I don't say why I'm there. I just need to watch her for a few minutes, and sometimes I need to talk to her. And she's just in her own world, maybe cleaning something or putting away the groceries and she'll say, 'Well, that's done' and ask me about my day and everything becomes normal and safe again. I don't like her knowing I feel this way. Not because I'm ashamed exactly, but it would really give her the wrong idea about how I feel in general. Because in general I'm fine. I don't need her, and I'm very independent. It's hard enough to make her see all that, without messing things up by showing that I need her, too.

And Cassie, at fifteen, says:

When I hear Mom is going to be out, at first I feel really pleased. The place all to myself! But when I get into bed, I keep listening to all those sounds—there are these creaking and whooshing noises, and I can get as frightened as I ever did as a kid. When I hear her come in, there's this rush of relief. Of course I don't say anything, and I let her think I'm asleep, but it's hard to fall asleep when she's not at home.

The very difficult balance is clear. The demanding daughter wants her independence, but needs connection. She wants her mother to respect her growth and maturity and independence, but not yet to let go.

## Attachment and Dependence

The "dependence" in which adult daughters continue to "need" mothers, is not a "dependence" in which they fail to achieve capacity for independent action and thought. It is a dependence formed through attachment, through the need to sustain the connection, and to maintain its good working order. The Mommy's girl that continues to live inside the feisty teen does not diminish her maturity, but contributes to her individuality, as someone with a history of changing and abiding relationships. The growing daughter is acknowledging continuity rather than regression when she says she still needs her mother.

A strong bond with a mother is not just for girls. Grace Baruch and Rosalind Barnett studied the conditions under which adult women thrive.[1] They asked whether the women between the ages of thirty-five and fifty-five, were generally happier if they remained close to a mother. Or, were women who felt distant and separate from a mother in some ways better off? Baruch and Barnett found that adult women were psychologically better off when they had good relations with their mothers: They had higher self-esteem, felt less anxious, less depressed than did women who were at odds with their mothers. Not only did they benefit from good relations, but they also valued them—and at the same time they valued them, they knew that their continuing love and persistent "dependence," were unfashionable: "I know it sounds silly," admitted one woman who said that when she felt down, she still, at forty, felt comforted by being with her mother. Often mothers were seen by adult daughters as a source of comfort, and, even in maturity, the mother was "a primary person from whom affirmation is sought."[2]

The lifelong attachment to one's mother continues to make a difference to a daughter's well-being, but the nature of this attachment shifts. During adolescence she individuates herself from the mother, seeking, discovering, and forging differences, while she watches out for, anticipates, and criticizes her mother's and father's responses, seeking a sign that her developing self is validated through their (positive or negative) responses, or legitimized through their admiration and understanding.[3] Much of the tension that frequently characterizes mother/daughter relationships during adolescence is linked to this special love and need; for it is through her love for her mother that a daughter is sensitive to conversational disappointments and frustrations. However different she becomes from her mother, or from the adolescent girl who developed through her mother, her mother's responses remain a significant point of reference.

The independent identity a daughter seeks never sets hard. In her early adult years she often checks up on it, expecting to find that it has. The internal persistence of the maternal gaze is experienced as an intrusion: "Why doesn't my mother leave me alone?" she protests, as she hears, inside her own head, her mother's voice. What often releases further energy is another shift as she realizes in midlife that the maternal gaze and voice are permanent and potentially valuable parts of her, just as they will be for her daughter.

## Unfounded Expectations of Independence

According to imbedded myths about maturity, our feelings for our parents in adulthood should be cleansed of adolescent anger, resentment, and ambivalence. A common expectation is that once we are really grown-up, our parents shrink to human size, and we (supposedly) no longer expect or need so much from these ordinary mortals, and therefore no longer brood over their failure to give us just what we need.

But that intense psychological bond with a mother does not dissolve as we grow up. Sharon, Enola, Bridget, Vicky, Robyn—women who are learning the steps necessary in negotiations with a teenage daughter—are still learning the steps necessary to deal with their own mothers. Bridget feels a rush of anger as her mother praises her sister's daughter's manners, and then she feels guilty for being brusque with a woman who had been so happy to see her. Enola says her mother still blames her for the breakup of the marriage, and at every meeting, braces herself for the maternal grilling about her love life. Sharon dreads passing on to her mother the news of her daughter's academic setbacks, and hearing, whether or not the words were actually spoken, criticism of her parenting style. "What is so surprising," Sharon says, "is how similar it all is today with how it was in my teens."

The dynamics of dealing with their own daughters bring

home to them how unfair or difficult they had been as teens, how worried their mothers had been on their behalf, and how long lasting is the impact of a mother's words. "Do I give my daughter as much cause for complaint as my mother has given me?" Bridget wonders, and Sharon says, "I want Becky to respect what I say, but not to be afraid of me like I was of my mother." And Vicky says, "I want Alex to trust herself and feel that, whatever she decides to do, I'm rooting for her. I don't want her to hear my angry words inside her brain."

The process by which we disengage from this passionate and productive conflict is gradual and piecemeal and never complete. We achieve an ability to function as though we were fully independent of them, but there remain hot underground springs of child-emotion that, in various circumstances, gush forth, unadulterated by maturity. The steps set in the mother/teenage daughter dance are needed throughout our lives.

The process of differentiating oneself from one's mother is a lifelong task. Pippa says that she "could not be more different from my mother. We have different views on almost everything. But still I find myself thinking that I'm doing just what she would do. Every day, there will be some little thing I say or do that makes me think I'm just like her, after all." And still, these independent women, themselves mothers of teenagers, seek their own mothers' approval. "Whenever I have a really good piece of news, I look forward to telling her. Then, if she's not as pleased as I think she should be I get so mad! And she'll say, 'What are you fussing about?' And, really, I feel stupid, because it's crazy why I care so much," Enola muses. "But with her, I can still be me at seven, wanting that big smile shining on me to feel whole."

As adults, we continue to seek a mother's approval, and continue to criticize the approval she offers, because it isn't quite right, quite to the point, or quite what we wanted in the first place. As soon as we feel ready to forgive a mother for some past transgression, we find ourselves at her throat again, complaining of a look, a turn of phrase, an assumption or expectation that threatens the stability of our hard-won ground.

But our continuing battle is not always directed against the mother's current attempts to constrain or control her, or to fashion her in some idealized daughter image. Instead, it is against all the mothers we have experienced in our past—the mother upon whom we were dependent as infants for life itself, the mother who seemed so powerful when we were children, the mother whose judgment we feared and then resented in adolescence. Robyn addresses sifted, collated memories rather than actual speech when she deals with what she calls a "shadow voice" sounding her mother's disapproval as she reprimands an employee ("You can be cold, girl"), or buys an expensive pair of boots ("Do you really need those?"). And, then, in the midst of our continuing battle, we discover her final triumph—the sound of her voice in ours as we speak. "I shout at Gemma, and I hear my mother's words come out of my mouth."

Mothers play many useful roles: as model, advisor, supporter—and antagonist. Pippa came to know her own individual vision by contrasting it with her mother's. Enola, even today, defines her own personal goals by distinguishing them from those of her mother: "I keep arguing with her, you know, carrying on these arguments inside my head, and gathering all the evidence I can that women can be good mothers without a man, that they can raise great kids with-

out a father around, and that a divorced woman isn't necessarily a lonely woman."

The crux of that long "adolescent" task is not a freeing of
the daughter's psyche from the mother's but an acknowledgment that "some part of her is forever imbedded" within us,
and "we are not the worse for it."[4] The supplementary realization seems to be that we were focusing on the surface all
along, and that the real depths of our mother's impact, which
we felt so familiar with, were in fact hidden by our preoccupation with minor irritations. We do not win an adolescent
battle but accept the fluid boundaries between her and us,
which gradually become less threatening, as our sense of self
becomes more layered and flexible. The battle is over when
we acknowledge the connection, and its implacable perma-
nence, but no longer feel bound and constrained by it.

## Motherless Daughters

A teen's relationship with her mother shapes her growth
through adolescence. Girls find various ways to test and
define themselves, always using a mother as a point of reference, always working to shave and hone her responses to
their changing self. What then happens when a girl loses her
developmental coach and partner? What happens when a
teenage girl does not have a mother? What happens when a
mother dies?

A child's loss of her mother touches us beyond words. A
monumental shift occurs in a motherless child's life; much
of the child's world will appear the same, yet is utterly transformed. It is, however, only during the teenage years that
the capacity to grieve is fully developed. The loss of a parent
has a profound impact on very young children, but a pre-

teen's response does not take the shape of what we think of as mourning. Unable to hold in their minds the image of a person, and to register the finality of death, young children suffer as much as teens but experience a more piecemeal and undigested grief. A teenager is mentally equipped to comprehend the loss, confront it, accept it, and move forward.

But this is difficult.

The impact of losing a mother is lifelong. Clare, now thirty, lost her mother when she was fifteen, but "the day she died seems like yesterday, or maybe more like a parallel today. There's something that hasn't ever changed since that day. It's like it just happened and is still happening."

She does not feel like crying as she once did, but she still misses her mother and keeps coming up against gaps that she believes would be filled in women who have mothers. "I think of all the little things I don't know, because she didn't teach me. There will be these things other women know, and I feel I don't because my mom wasn't there to tell me or show me. I was never properly fitted for a bra until last year when I thought about it and realized, 'This is ridiculous!' But other things aren't so easy. I know my mom was a good cook, and I remember her doing stuff in the kitchen, but I don't remember the details. When I'm trying to make something and it goes wrong, I think, 'Why did she have to die?'"

When Clare catches sight of her mother's qualities in other people, she experiences an immediate connection. She describes her husband as "being a lot like my mom in some ways, something about his smile and the kind of surprised look on his face, just before he laughs, when I say something funny. But I still miss her, and still feel I'm missing something because I don't have her. I think how sad it will be if I have children and she won't see them."

As an adult who has had a long time to reflect on the meaning of her loss, Clare's regret, though strong, is controlled. For a teen, annoyance can mix with grief. "Why does my life have to be messed around?" is a question Fran, sixteen, asks, when her mother dies following a surgery that was expected to be routine. She wants to return to her normal routine and is disturbed to see that her friends and teachers have changed toward her.

> I walked into school, and suddenly there were all these people surrounding me like I was some freak everyone had to pity. "How are you?" they wanted to know. "Are you okay?" "Is there anything we can do?" Even my math teacher, whom I really loathe, lurched toward me like she wanted to hug me. I hated it that they'd all been talking about me and that they knew about something that seemed to be happening in a very different place. For some reason it didn't occur to me they would know about it, that they would talk about it. And I was furious. What business is it of theirs? So I just said, "I'm fine. Why shouldn't I be fine?" and I went to my locker and took of my coat and got my books. I didn't see how any words I used could explain what I felt.

Bereft, but also ambivalent, Fran wants her own life back. She wants to be who she was and she resents the entire business of her mother's death because it transforms her in others' eyes into an object of pity. While teens often cry in anger, they prefer not to weep with grief, especially in front of grown-ups, whose responses make them feel "babyish." When their grief is profound, it is also terrifying, and letting go threatens them with confrontation of the magnitude of their emotions. Teenage girls who appear to be "coping" or "taking it well" are often simply frozen in fear.

The twist of grief's knife for a teen who loses her mother

is that she sees perhaps the thread of relief (No more hassle from an overprotective, intrusive mother!) or selfish resentment (Why does all this funeral and family stuff have to mess me up?) in her braided emotions. Tamsin, fourteen, whose mother died after a long illness, takes a cool look at both her loss and her gain. Having witnessed her mother's panic at the initial diagnoses, comforted her when her hair came out in tufts, persuaded her to eat when racked by nausea, Tamsin admits: "When she died I thought, 'I don't have to go through that anymore.'" She could move about the house, listen to music, watch television, shout and cry, without hearing the whispered directive, "Don't disturb your mother."

But when a mother dies, teenage girls often experience new constraints. The mothers in this study frequently tried to protect a daughter from being cast into a typical female role. "How about your making it yourself," Joyce gently chides Greg when he asks Naomi to make him a sandwich. "I'll get that. She just sat down," Pam told her son who asked Margot to fetch the bicycle pump she had borrowed. "She looks fine!" Meg's mother insisted when Alan asked her whether she was "really planning to go out looking like that." But when a mother dies, the family dynamics change, and a teen does not have a mother to deflect others' expectations of what she, as a young woman, should do and how she should look.

Many teenage girls who lose their mothers do become "the woman of the house." Fran said she felt sorry for her father, and was worried because he was crying, and she had never seen him cry, and though that made her want to cry, she felt it would worry her younger sister and brother unduly. Her aunt told her to "be brave and look after your father." While there was now no one to "judge me and tell me what I should do," there was also "no one around to take care of us and remind everyone that I need my space."

In her book *Motherless Daughters: The Legacy of Loss*, Hope Edelman describes how within eight days of her mother's death she "stepped on a fast-forward button that transported [her] from seventeen to forty-two." She began driving her brothers to their haircuts, taking her sister to the dentist, and carrying the household's incidental cash in her wallet.[5] A mother's presence protects a girl from the burden of these roles, partly because a mother herself tends to take on these roles, and partly because mothers tend to monitor a fair division of emotional work and housework.

It is through a dynamic dialogue with a mother that girls normally develop. Without such a dialogue, it is difficult for all parts of a girl to grow. Hope Edelman says that when her mother died, part of her raced to the age of forty-two, part of her remained stuck at seventeen, and the rest developed along normal lines. Motherless daughters find other ways to pick up knowledge and to develop. They may imagine a mother's voice and carry on an internal dialogue. They may find aspects of a mother in friends, partners, and mentors, with whom they pick up the conversation. The legacy of a mother's death is loss, but the internal dialogue with a mother is so persistent that, in some sense, we never lose her.

At different points in adulthood, daughters frame the prospect of a parent's death in very different ways and concentrate on different aspects of their loss. In one study of women reflecting on their aging parents,[6] a woman in her thirties said that without her parents, she would be lost: "They've helped me through many, many hard times. I really wouldn't know what to do [if they died]. I don't even want to talk about them leaving because I just want them around forever. I just kind of block that right out of my mind. When my father had the heart attack, it scared me half to death."[7]

These women still speak of parents in terms of their own need for them. They long to talk to them, to hear them speak "straight out and tell [them] what they think," and they are still dependent on a mother as a resource for strength and comfort. Sharon, at forty-two, recalls her response to her own mother's bereavement at her grandmother's death: "My mom's mom died, when she was forty, and I found her panic unwholesomely dramatic. Her grief was flung at me like a brick. I could not understand what she was grieving for. Her mother was a problem. They argued constantly. Every meeting was followed by a new spate of criticism. Yet she was inconsolable."

In fact, only well into midlife do women contemplate the death of a mother in terms of a disinterested hope that she will die happy, without pain or discomfort or regret: "I hope that she won't be uncomfortable," a fifty-year-old woman reflects. "And I hope that she will just go and not be frightened at the time . . . If they told me that she would die tomorrow, I think I'd be very, very happy because I'd know that she had a happy life to the last moment."[8]

In midlife, the battle that began in adolescence can be put to rest, and the need that makes this relationship so powerful and so tense can be eased into a disinterested love. And yet—beneath these healthy shifts in mourning remains a daughter's abiding child-love. Even the most independent woman, well established in midlife, can experience a child-terror at a parent's death. When Pauline Perry spoke in public about her violent, unanticipated grief at her mother's death, she was flooded with responses from other women who, in their fifties and sixties, shared her feelings.[9] They, too, felt that no preparation for such a loss was possible, and that abiding grief at a mother's death was inevitable at any age.

Several women described a sense of "panic" or "terror" when their mothers died. Pam, forty-five, said that she walked out of the hospital, having made the arrangements for her mother's burial, and longed to embrace "every kind-faced person on the street" to gain comfort. She felt "help-less," and kept forgetting she was grown-up and independent: "I might as well have been ten years old—those were the feelings I had. I kept seeing myself as ten, and not having a mother to go home to." Thea, forty-three, said that she kept hearing her mother call out to her, "like she's asking for my help and I can't give it to her because I don't know where she is." The twin fears of being abandoned and of being the abandoner haunted their period of grief. And when the intensity of mourning subsided, they were left with a changed self, a self that they now felt had been pushed into true middle age, decidedly mortal.

In speaking about their grief, women in their forties still revealed how closely they saw themselves and defined themselves in relation to their mothers. Bridget said, "I spent so much time countering what she would say, pinpointing the ways she was undermining me—what picky fights we had! Now I have that noninterference I was fighting for! Much good it all does me. My thoughts drip into an empty bucket. No resonance."

As much as we complain about the conflict with a mother, we often need it to feel cared for and grounded. Delia, whose mother died during the course of my interviews with her and her daughter, reflected, "I fought her for so long, far longer than was necessary. I had already got the independence I'd wanted. I pushed her away because she seemed threatening to me, long after she really was. If she had lived for a few years longer, I might have been able to learn this before it was too late for me to share it with her. I was just beginning to feel it—the end of that long adolescent resistance. I regret being unable to offer this forgiveness."

## Lifelong Negotiations

And yet there is one sense in which we never lose a mother. Even when we cannot argue with her, face-to-face, even when she becomes an elderly woman, disengaged from the battles we continue to seek with her, we retain that internal dialogue.

Several milestones change a woman's relationship with her mother. Distinctive events can be experienced as marking out a new balance. Sexual initiation, marriage, or pregnancy may make a daughter feel part of that women's club and give her new access to a mother's previously mysterious knowledge. Sometimes a new job, a promotion, a success, or even a new home is viewed partly in terms of what it should mean to her mother, and what status, vis-à-vis a mother, it gives her. Sometimes a daughter makes such a claim to equality, only to be reminded that the distance between the two women has not changed. "I came home for a visit after I'd been working in Denver for eight months," Lan, now twenty-two complains, "and there was my mother treating me as though I couldn't cross the street safely unless she hurtled advice after me."

While daughters, well into adulthood, often expect some

change within themselves to effect a sudden, dramatic change in their relationship with their mothers, negotiations in the relationship often remain piecemeal and gradual. Painstakingly, and often with irritation at her slow pupil, the adult daughter "teaches" the mother precisely what a new role or new position or new achievement or direction means. Sometimes the roles the daughter takes are very different from what the mother expected or even what she, having come to adulthood in a different time, thought possible. Many women whose mothers never thought of working outside their home, who never conceived of achievement outside traditional female roles, still try to offer up their own professional achievements as a gift. This offering, with its abiding supposition that achievement is given depth and reality through a parent's endorsement, is often spiked with criticism. The parent—so the child judges—has not been sufficiently impressed, or pleased, or appreciative. A daughter who wants a very different life from her mother's is no less concerned to gain her mother's attention and appreciation than is a woman who chooses her mother as a role model. Both women who admire their mother's lifestyle and life choices and those who feel highly critical of a mother's values and choices, have to work toward release from concerns about pleasing her or impressing her.

The relationship between midlife women and their mothers is a modern phenomenon, brought about by increased life expectancy.[10] Vicky, facing difficulties with her own daughter, reflects in new ways on an old relationship. "I gave her hell when I was a teenager, and now I look at her and just can't see what I saw then. I thought she was my jailer, and I thought she was standing in my way. That's all I saw of her—some great big shadow blocking my path. And now when I feel how mild she is—well, I look at her and suddenly my heart will start thumping because I get afraid when I think of how I used to rage against her. Sometimes I think she's expecting me to light into her like I used to. It's just—you turn around and suddenly she's a different person. I want to show her that I'm grateful she's stood by me, and didn't give up hope that one day I might say a nice word or two to her."

For some women, the need to keep close and get closer involves the wish to rediscover the mother and to explore her perspective and, through their voices, validate their mothers' lives anew. Looking back on her childhood, Bridget expresses a new curiosity about what things were like for her mother, how her hopes had been formed and then transformed, and what role she, as daughter, played in fulfilling or hindering those hopes. Lisette initiates new discussions with her sister and brother to help her reconstruct the neglected drama of her mother's life. "I spent many hours telling her what was wrong with her life," Lisette realizes. "Maybe it's time now I let her speak for herself."

But for their adolescent daughters, there is still a road ahead. Just beyond adolescence, in her early twenties, Lan lists her new adult achievements, and notes how surprised her mother is, and pleased, and what a crucial role her mother's responses play in her life. She remains touchy about the surprise, and rewarded by the pride. "Here I am," reflects Lan, "living on my own, and managing life pretty well on my own. But a hundred times a day I'll find myself talking to her, as though she's here, arguing with me."

Mothers and daughters continue to quarrel because neither gives up on the other. Underlying the continuing quarrels is the hope that, this time, she will get the right response, and have the final say in her battle for a mother's recognition. This bond is due not only, and perhaps not primarily, to the biological dependence of infancy but also to the intimate dynamics of her adolescent development within this relationship.

The mark of being really grown-up, in relation to one's mother, is not severing the bond between them, but accepting it as part of her identity. A teenage girl grows into a woman still puzzled by that tricky equation between her own identity and that of her mother, and still prepared to fight one more battle to make their different positions clear. Moments of enlightenment, when she feels the history of herself in that relationship, gradually extend to appreciation, as that relationship becomes a bedrock of her emotional and psychological history.

# *Notes*

**INTRODUCTION**

1. David Bell and Linda Bell, "Parental validation and Support in the Development of Adolescent Daughters," in *Adolescent Development in the Family*, ed. Harold Grotevant and Catherine Cooper (San Francisco: Jossey-Bass, 1985); James Youniss and Jacqueline Smollar, *Adolescent Relations with Mothers, Fathers and Friends* (Chicago: University of Chicago Press, 1985).

2. Janet Surrey, "The Mother-Daughter relationship: Themes in Psychotherapy," in *Daughtering and Mothering: Female Subjectivity Reanalyzed* (New York: Routledge, 1993), 115.

3. Jane Smith, "Mothers: Tired of Taking the Rap," *New York Times Magazine*, 142, 17.

4. Janet Surrey, op. cit. 122.

5. Elizabeth Debold, Marie Wilson, and Idelisse Malave, *The Mother/Daughter Revolution* (New York: Bantam, 1994).

**CHAPTER ONE**

1. Lynne Murray and Colwyn Trvarthen, "Emotional Regulation of Interaction Between Two-Month-Olds and Their Mothers," in *Social Perception in Infants*, ed. T.M. Fields and N.A. Fox (Norwood, N.J: Ablex Publishing, 1985).

2. Marion Forgatch and Gerald Patterson, *Parents and Adolescents: Living Together*, part 2 (Eugene, Oreg.: Castalia, 1989), 10.

3. Deborah Tannen, *You Just Don't Understand* (New York: Morrow, 1990).

4. Rachel Simmons, *Odd Girl Out: The Hidden Culture of Aggression in Girls* (New York: Harcourt, 2002); Rosalind Wiseman, *Queen Bees and Wannabees: Helping Your Daughter Survive Cliques, Gossip, Boyfriends and Other Realities of Adolescence* (New York: Crown, 2002); Terri Apter and Ruthellen Josselson, *Best Friends: The Pleasures and Perils of Girls' and Women's Friendships* (New York: Crown, 1998).

5. Luise Eichenbaum and Susie Orbach, *Between Women: Love, Envy and Competition in Women's Friendships* (New York: Anchor, 1990)

## CHAPTER TWO

1. Anna Freud, "Adolescence," in *The Psychoanalytic Study of the Child*, vol. 13 (New York: International Universities Press, 1958), 255–78. See also, Peter Blos, *The Adolescent Passage* (New York: International Universities Press, 1979)

2. Harold Grotevant and Catherine Cooper, op.cit.

3. Margaret Mahler, "Thoughts about Development and Individuation," in *The Psychoanalytic Study of the Child*, vol. 18 (New York: International Universities Press, 1963), 307-24; M. Mahler, F. Pine, and A. Bergman, *The Psychological Birth of the Human Infant* (New York: Basic Books, 1975).

4. As Anne Frank wrote, "I hid myself within myself . . . and quietly wrote down all my joys, sorrows, and contempt in my diary."

5. Lyn Mikel Brown, *Raising Their Voices: The Politics of Girls' Anger* (Cambridge, Mass: Harvard University Press, 1998).

6. Quoted in Nancy Snyderman and Peg Streep, *The Girl in the Mirror: Mothers and Daughters in the Years of Adolescence* (New York: Hyperion, 2001), 103.

7. The anthropologist Gregory Bateson identified and named this process as "complementary schismogenesis." Gregory Bateson, *Steps to an Ecology of Mind* (New York: Ballantine, 1972).

8. David Bell and Linda Bell, op.cit.
9. See John Gottman, *Why Marriages Succeed or Fail* (New York: Simon and Schuster, 1994).

**CHAPTER THREE**

1. Diane Baumrind, "Current Patterns of Parental Authority," *Developmental Psychology Monographs* 4 (1,2); see also, Terri Apter, *The Confident Child* (New York: Norton, 1998).
2. David Elkind, *The Hurried Child: Growing Up Too Fast Too Soon* (Reading, Mass: Addison-Wesley, 1981).
3. Jay Giedd et al., "Brain Development During Childhood and Adolescence: A Longitudinal MRI Study," *Nature Neuroscience*, 2, 861; Elizabeth R. Sowell et al., "In Vivo Evidence for Post-Adolescent Brain Maturation in Frontal and Striatal Regions," *Nature Neuroscience*, 2, 859.
4. Barbara Strauch, *Why Are They So Weird?* (London: Bloomsbury, 2003).
5. See Terri Apter, *Altered Loves: Mothers and Daughters During Adolescence*, chap. 6 (New York: Fawcett, 1991).
6. Terri Apter, *Secret Paths: Women in the New Midlife* (New York: Norton, 1997).
7. Lynn Ponton, *The Romance of Risk* (New York: Basic Books, 1997).

**CHAPTER FOUR**

1. Erik Erikson, *Identity, Youth and Crisis* (New York: Norton, 1968).

**CHAPTER FIVE**

1. See Carol Gilligan, *The Birth of Pleasure: A New Map of Love* (New York: Knopf, 2002), 31.
2. Marion Forgatch and Gerald Patterson, vol. 1, op. cit., 40.

**CHAPTER SIX**

1. See, for example, Majorie Harness Goodwin, *He-Said-She-Said: Talk as Social Organization Among Black Children* (Bloomington:

Indiana University Press, 1991); Penelope Eckert, "Cooperative Competition in Adolescent 'Girl Talk,'" *Discourse Process* 13:1; Rachel Simmons, *Odd Girl Out: The Hidden Culture of Aggression in Girls* (New York: Harcourt, 2002); Rosalind Wiseman, *Queen Bees and Wannabees: Helping Your Daughter Survive Cliques, Gossip, Boyfriends and Other Realities of Adolescence* (New York: Crown, 2002).

2. Terri Apter and Ruthellen Josselson, *Best Friends: The Pleasures and Perils of Girls' and Women's Friendships* (New York: Crown, 1998).

## CHAPTER SEVEN

1. Gerald Patterson and Marion Forgatch, "The Basics," pt. 1 of *Parents and Adolescents: Living Together* (Eugene, Ore.: Castalia Publishing Company, 1987).

2. Ibid., vol. 1.

## CHAPTER EIGHT

1. Terri Apter, *Altered Loves: Mothers and Daughters During Adolescence* (New York: Fawcett, 1991).

2. Deborah Tannen, *You Just Don't Understand* (New York: Morrow, 1990).

3. James Youniss and Jacqueline Smollar, *Adolescent Relations with Mothers, Fathers and Friends* (Chicago: University of Chicago Press, 1985).

4. Deborah Tannen, op. cit., 42

5. Amy Sheldon, "Pickle Fights: Gendered Talk in Preschool Disputes," *Discourse Processes* 13:1,cited in Tannen, op. cit., 45.

6. John Gottman with Nan Silver, *Why Marriages Succeed or Fail* (New York: Fireside, 1994).

7. Terri Apter, *Secret Paths: Women in the New Midlife* (New York: Norton, 1995).

8. Eirini Flouir and Ann Buchanan, "Father Involvement and Outcomes in Adolescence and Adulthood," *End of Award Report*

(Oxford: Economic and Social Research Council, October 24, 2001).

9. Girls tend to feel close to involved fathers, but they are close to a mother whether or not they describe her as involved. (See Judy Dunn and Kirby Deater-Deckard, *Children's Views of Their Changing Families* (Layerthorpe, New York: Joseph Rowntree Foundation, 2002).

## CHAPTER NINE

1. Terri Apter and Ruthellen Josselson, op. cit.
2. Mimi Nichter, *Fat Talk: What Girls and Their Parents Say About Dieting* (Cambridge, Mass.: Harvard University Press, 2000).
3. Joan Jacobs Brumberg, *The Body Project: An Intimate History of American Girls* (New York: Random House, 1997).
4. Dr Katherine Halmi, director of the eating disorders program at the Westchester division of New York–Presbyterian Hospital; in a Swedish study that followed patients for thirty years, 18 to 20 percent of the women died.
5. Bryan Lask and Rachel Bryant-Waugh, eds., *Anorexia nervosa and related eating disorders in childhood and adolescence* (Hove, England: Psychology Press, 2000).
6. Traditional theories of anorexia hold that self-starvation is a teenager's desperate attempt to assert independence from overbearing parents, particularly a mother; as a result, parents were directed not to participate in treatment. Current theories recognize that the most effective treatment involves parental participation. James Locke, *Treatment Manual for Anorexia Nervosa: A Family-Based Approach* (New York: Guildford Press, 2002).
7. While some psychologists believe that to blame the media is to trivialize life-threatening psychiatric illnesses, it does seem that the pressure is sufficient to push 2 percent of the population over the edge of what we now think of as a normal concern about weight to pathology. see Rhona MacDonald, "To Diet For:

Are the Media to Blame for Eating Disorders?" *British Medical Journal* 322:1002 (21 April 2001).

8. In a study involving a racially mixed group of 240 American girls, aged fourteen to sixteen years, almost 90 percent of the white girls were dissatisfied with their body shape (although 80 percent were actually normal weight for their height), 70 percent of the African-American girls were satisfied or very satisfied with their current weight and considered themselves attractive—even if they happened to be (as 18 percent were) overweight by biomedical standards. African-American girls looked at their bodies with a dynamic dimension and talked about girls "who know what to do with themselves" rather than girls who were beautiful by some static standard. see Mimi Nichter, op.cit.

## CHAPTER TEN

1. Sharon Thompson, "Putting a Big Thing Into a Little Hole," *Journal of Sex Research*, no. 3 (27 August 1990): 341–61.

2. Ibid.

3. According to a Carnegie Council report (1995), by the age of seventeen, about a quarter of all adolescents have engaged in behaviors that are harmful or dangerous to themselves and others: getting pregnant, using drugs, taking part in antisocial activity, and failing in school. Altogether, nearly half of American adolescents are at high or moderate risk of seriously damaging their life chances. Carnegie Council on Adolescent Development, *Great Transitions: Preparing Adolescents for a New Century* (New York: Carnegie Corporation, 1995).

4. Ibid.

5. In a survey of 750 girls between the ages of twelve and nineteen, 85 percent identified drinking as a major factor leading to sex. Lloyd Johnson, Patrick O'Malley, and Jerald Bachman, *National Survey Results on Drug Use from the Monitoring of the Future Study, 1975–1994* (Rockville, Md.: U.S. Department of Health and

Human Services, Public Health Service, National Institutes of Health, National Institute on Drug Use, 1995).

6. H. M Klein, *Love, Guilt, and Reparation and Other Works 1921–1945* (New York: Delta, 1975); D. W. Winnicott, *Through Paediatrics to Psychoanalysis* (New York: Basic Books, 1975); J. Benjamin, *The Bonds of Love: Psychoanalysis, Feminism and the Problem of Domination* (New York: Pantheon, 1988).

7. Nancy Chodorow, *The Reproduction of Mothering* (Berkeley, Calif.: University of California Press, 1978).

8. Deborah Tannen, *I Only Say This Because I Love You: How the Way We Talk Can Make or Break Family Relationships Throughout Our Lives* (New York: Random House, 2001), 196–98.

9. Natalie Bartle with Susan Lieberman, *Venus in Blue Jeans: Why Mothers and Daughters Need to Talk about Sex* (Boston and New York: Houghton Mifflin, 1998).

## CHAPTER ELEVEN

1. Carol Gilligan, *The Birth of Pleasure: A New Map of Love* (New York: Knopf, 2002), 108.

2. Anne Frank, *Diary*, 14 October 1942, cited in Gilligan, op.cit., 86. Gilligan notes that this passage was omitted by Anne when she edited her diary, and Otto Frank, in his editing, restored it.

3. Carol Gilligan, op. cit.

4. Elizabeth Debold, Marie Wilson, and Idelisse Malave, *The Mother/Daughter Revolution* (New York: Bantam, 1994).

## CHAPTER TWELVE

1. Grace Baruch and Rosalind Barnett, "Adult Daughters' Relationships with Their Mothers: The Era of Good Feelings," *Journal of Marriage and the Family* 45 (1983): 601–6.

2. Ibid., 347; Ruthellen Jossleson, 1987, also found that the adult women she interviewed continued to feel close to a mother and valued a friendly relationship.

3. For an extensive analysis of this process see Terri Apter, *Altered*

Loves: Mothers and Daughters During Adolescence (New York: St. Martin's, 1990); for an account of validation, see David Bell and Linda Bell, op. cit.

4. Ibid., 383.
5. Hope Edelman, Motherless Daughters: The Legacy of Loss (London: Hodder, 1995), 452.
6. Anne Stueve and Lydia O'Donnell, "The Daughter of Aging Parents," in Grace Baruch and Jeanne Brooks-Gunn, eds., Women in Midlife (New York: Plenum Press, 1984), 203–25.
7. Ibid., 211.
8. Ibid.
9. Pauline Perry, The Womb in Which I Lay (London: Souvenir Press, 2003).
10. Though men now live longer, extending the time they may have in relationships with adult children, women live longer than men, and the differential in life expectancy is increasing. For every 100 elderly women there are only 69 elderly men. This differential has increased since the beginning of the century—when there were 102 men sixty-five years or older for every 100 women. In 1960 there were 83 men for every 100 women, and in 1975 there were 60 men for 100 women. see Anne Stueve and Lydia O'Donnell, op. cit., 203–25.

# Bibliography

Apter, Terri. *Altered Loves: Mothers and Daughters During Adolescence.* New York: Fawcett, 1991.

———. *Secret Paths: Women in the New Midlife.* New York: Norton, 1995.

———. *The Confident Child.* New York: Norton, 1998.

Apter, Terri, and Ruthellen Josselson. *Best Freinds: The Pleasures and Perils of Girls' and Women's Friendships.* New York: Crown, 1998.

Bartle, Natalie, with Susan Lieberman. *Venus in Blue Jeans: Why Mothers and Daughters Need to Talk About Sex.* Boston and New York: Houghton Mifflin, 1998.

Baruch, Grace, and Rosalind Barnett. "Adult Daughters' Relationships with Their Mothers: The Era of Good Feelings." *Journal of Marriage and the Family* 45 (1983): 601–6

Bateson, Gregory. *Steps to an Ecology of Mind.* New York: Ballantine, 1972.

Baumrind, Diane. "Current Patterns of Parental Authority." *Developmental Psychology Monographs* 4 (1,2).

Bell, David, and Linda Bell. "Parental Validation and Support in the Development of Adolescent Daughters." In *Adolescent Development in the Family,* edited by Harold Grotevant and Catherine Cooper. San Francisco: Jossey-Bass, 1983.

Benjamin, Jessica. *The Bonds of Love: Psychoanalysis, Feminism and the Problem of Domination.* New York: Pantheon, 1988.

Blos, Peter. *The Adolescent Passage.* New York: International Universities Press, 1979.

Brown, Lyn Mikel. *Raising Their Voices: The Politics of Girls' Anger.* Cambridge, Mass: Harvard University Press, 1998.

Brumberg, Joan Jacobs. *The Body Project: An Intimate History of American Girls.* New York: Random House, 1997.

Carnegie Council on Adolescent Development. *Great Transitions: Preparing Adolescents for a New Century.* New York: Carnegie Corporation, 1995.

Chodorow, Nancy. *The Reproduction of Mothering.* Berkeley, Calif.: University of California Press, 1978.

Debold, Elizabeth, Marie Wilson, and Idelisse Malave. *The Mother/Daughter Revolution.* New York: Bantam, 1994.

Dunn, Judy, and Kirby Deater-Deckard. *Children's Views of their Changing Families.* Layerthorpe, York: Joseph Rowntree, 2002.

Eckert, Penelope. "Cooperative Competition in Adolescent 'Girl Talk.'" *Discourse Process* 13:1 (1990).

Edelman, Hope. *Motherless Daughters: The Legacy of Loss.* London: Hodder, 1995, 452.

Eichenbaum, Luise, and Susie Orbach. *Between Women: Love, Envy and Competition in Women's Friendships.* New York: Anchor, 1990.

Elkind, David. *The Hurried Child: Growing Up Too Fast Too Soon.* Reading, Mass: Addison-Wesley, 1981.

Erikson, Erik. *Identity, Youth and Crisis.* New York: Norton, 1968.

Flouir, Eirini, and Ann Buchanan. "Father Involvement and Outcomes in Adolescence and Adulthood." *End of Award Report.* Oxford: Economic and Social Research Council, October 24, 2001.

Frank, Anne. *Diary.*

Freud, Anna. 1958. "Adolescence." In *The Psychoanalytic Study of the Child*, vol. 13, 255–78.

Giedd, Jay et al. "Brain Development During Childhood and Adolescence: A Longitudinal MRI Study." *Nature Neuroscience* 2, 861.

Gilligan, Carol. *The Birth of Pleasure: A New Map of Love*. New York: Knopf, 2002.

Goodwin, Marjorie Harness. *He-Said-She-Said: Talk as Social Organization Among Black Children*. Bloomington: Indiana University Press, 1991.

Gottman, John, with Nan Silver. *Why Marriages Succeed or Fail*. New York: Fireside, 1994.

Johnson, Lloyd, Patrick O'Malley, and Jerald Bachman. *National Survey Results on Drug Use from the Monitoring the Future Study, 1975–1994*. Rockville, Md.: U.S. Department of Health and Human Services, Public Health Service, National Institutes of Health, National Institute on Drug Use, 1995.

Josselson, Ruthellen. *Finding Herself: Pathways to Identity in Women*. San Fransisco: Jossey-Bass, 1987.

Klein, Melanie. *Love, Guilt, and Reparation and Other Works 1921–1945*. New York: Delta, 1975.

Lask, Bryan, and Rachel Bryant-Waugh, eds. *Anorexia Nervosa and Related Eating Disorders in Childhood and Adolescence*. Hove, England: Psychology Press, 2000.

Locke, James. *Manual for Treating Anorexia*. New York: Guildford Press, 2002.

MacDonald, Rhona. "To Diet For: Are the Media to Blame for Eating Disorders?" *British Medical Journal* 322:1002 (21 April 2001).

Mahler, Margaret. "Thoughts about Development and Individuation." *The Psychoanalytic Study of the Child*, vol. 18, 307–24.

Mahler, Margaret, F. Pine, and A. Bergman. *The Psychological Birth of the Human Infant*. New York: Basic Books, 1975.

Murray, Lynne, and Colwyn Trvarthen. "Emotional Regulation of Interaction Between Two-Month-Olds and Their Mothers." In *Social Perception in Infants*, edited by T.M. Fields and N.A. Fox. Norwood, N.J: Ablex Publishing, 1985.

Nichter, Mimi. *Fat Talk: What Girls and Their Parents Say about Dieting*. Cambridge, Mass.: Harvard University Press, 2000.

Patterson, Gerald, and Marion Forgatch. "The Basics." Pt. 1 of *Parents and Adolescents: Living Together*. Eugene, Ore.: Castalia Publishing Company, 1987.

Ponton, Lynn. *The Romance of Risk: Why Teenagers Do the Things They Do*. New York: Basic Books, 1998.

Simmons, Rachel. *Odd Girl Out: The Hidden Culture of Aggression in Girls*. New York: Harcourt, 2002.

Smith, J. "Mothers: Tired of Taking the Rap". *New York Times Magazine*, 1 July 1990, 142, 17.

Snyderman, Nancy, and Peg Streep. *The Girl in the Mirror: Mothers and Daughters in the Years of Adolescence*. New York: Hyperion, 2001, 103.

Sowell, Elizabeth R., et al. "In Vivo Evidence for Post-Adolescent Brain Maturation in Frontal and Striatal Regions." *Nature Neuroscience* 2, 859.

Strauch, Barbara. *Why Are They So Weird?* London: Bloomsbury, 2003.

Stueve, Anne, and Lydia O'Donnell. "The Daughter of Aging Parents." In *Women in Midlife*, edited by Grace Baruch and Jeanne Brooks-Gunn. New York: Plenum Press, 1984, 203–25.

Surrey, Janet. "The Mother-Daughter Relationship: Themes in Psychotherapy." In *Daughtering and Mothering: Female Subjectivity Reanalyzed*. New York: Routledge, 1993, 115.

Tannen, Deborah. *I Only Say This Because I Love You: How the Way We Talk Can Make or Break Family Relationships Throughout Our Lives*. New York: Random House, 2001, 196–98.

——. *You Just Don't Understand*. New York: Morrow, 1990.

Thompson, Sharon. "Putting a Big Thing into a Little Hole." *Journal of Sex Research*, no. 3 (27 August 1990): 341–61.

Winnicott, Donald. *Through Pediatrics to Psychoanalysis*. New York: Basic Books, 1975.

Wiseman, Rosalind. *Queen Bees and Wannabees: Helping Your Daughter Survive Cliques, Gossip, Boyfriends and Other Realities of Adolescence*. New York: Crown, 2002.

Youniss, James, and Jacqueline Smollar. *Adolescent Relations with Mothers, Fathers and Friends*. Chicago: University of Chicago Press, 1985.

# Index

abandonment, fear of, 27, 239–41
  and loss of mother, 252
achievement of daughter, parent's
  endorsement of, 254
adolescence:
  changing relationships in, 18
  development in, 32
  distorted interpretations of behav-
    ior in, 8
  friendship wars in, 147–51
  mothers' concern with, 4–6
  poor judgment in, 70-73
  psychological theories of, 6–7
  *see also* father/daughter relation-
    ship; mother/daughter con-
    flict; mother/ daughter rela-
    tionship
adult women:
  attachment to mothers of, 241–46,
    254–56
  grief for lost mothers of, 247–48,
    251–52
advice, giving of, 24, 27
affection, demonstrations of,
  27
African-American girls, body image
  of, 262n
aggression, 127
  of daughters, 13
  hidden, 27

Aikido approach, 215
alienation, 54
alliance, and girls' conflict resolution, 171
*Altered Loves: Mothers and Daughters
  During Adolescence* (Apter), 7
anecdotal lying, 157–59
anger, 54, 55, 57–58
  acknowledgment of, 58, 228
  of daughters, 17, 25, 139, 184
  in early childhood, 221–22, 226
  of fathers, 168–70
  between mother and daughter,
    224, 225–26
  of mothers, 23, 25, 168, 235
  mothers' explanation of, 141
  offers of help and, 63–64
  peer conflict and, 149
  previous conflicts and, 127
  privacy violations and, 81
  of teenagers, 221–22, 225–26
anorexia, 187, 195–97, 261n
apologizing, 141
  by daughter to father, 167–68
appearance, hypersensitivity to,
  187–91
  *see also* weight, obsession with
appreciation:
  conflicts over, 17
  daughter's need for, 66